book should be return

shir

OTHER
PEOPLE'S
COUNTRIES

OTHER PEOPLE'S COUNTRIES

A Journey into Memory

Patrick McGuinness

JONATHAN CAPE

LONDON

Published by Jonathan Cape 2014

2 4 6 8 10 9 7 5 3 1

First published in Great Britain in 2014 by
Jonathan Cape
Random House, 20 Vauxhall Bridge Road,
London SW1V 2SA

www.randomhouse.co.uk

Addresses for companies within The Random House Group Limited can be found at:
www.randomhouse.co.uk/offices.htm

The Random House Group Limited Reg. No. 954009

A CIP catalogue record for this book is available from the British Library

ISBN 9780224098304

MIX
Paper fr
responsible
FSC
www.fsc.org   FSC® C0

Typeset by Palim

Printed and boun

For Osian and Mari, so they know where they come from

Allez, tais-toi, dit le paysage.
Come on, shut up, says the landscape.

PAUL DE ROUX

Contents

DRAMATIS PERSONAE

(The list does not include the living)

The Lejeunes, the Nicolas, the Bourlands and the McGuinnesses

Lucie Lejeune, née Nicolas, dressmaker, *couturière*, grandmother (1920–99)
Eugène Lejeune, 'Le Dènn', *ferronnier,* metalworker, grandfather (1914–83)

Monique Lejeune, mother (1942–2002)
Kevin McGuinness, father (1938–2004),
Collette Lejeune, aunt, teacher in the *école communale* (1944–87)

Paul Nicolas, great-uncle (1916–82)
Marie Nicolas, née Pierson (1918–2001)
Albert Nicolas, great-uncle (1912–96)
Emile Nicolas, great-uncle died in the fire of Bouillon (1911–44)

Julia Bourland, née Nicolas, great-grandmother, hotel chambermaid (1890–1975)
Elie Nicolas, great-grandfather, forest warden, husband of Julia Bourland, father of Lucie Lejeune (1890–1958)
Eugénie Bourland, great-great-aunt, sister of Julia, mother

of Victor Adam (1885–1971)

Lucie Bourland, great-great-aunt, seamstress (1889–1951)

Victor Adam ('Pistache'), father of Guy and brother of Nanette, executed by the Gestapo (1913–44)

Emile Lejeune ('Emile Picard', 'Emile la petite'), carter, great-grandfather, murdered in 'Le Maroc' (1882–1924)

Olga Lejeune, great aunt (1918–2000)

The Bouillonnais

Léon Degrelle, Belgian fascist leader (1906–94)

Edouard Degrelle, brother of Léon Degrelle, died aged twenty months (1902–4)

Edouard Degrelle, pharmacist and Léon Degrelle's brother, assassinated by unknown resistance members (1904–44)

Robert Hainaux, garagiste, bon-viveur and Fiat car salesman (1935–2007)

Marcel Hanus, 'Le Cul', 'L'Queu' ('The Arse'), café owner (1924–83)

'Mataba', Gaston Maziers, café owner (1906–84)

Maurice Pirotte, Bouillonnais poet and centenarian (1913–2013)

Madelaine Ozeray, actor (1908–89)

Godefroid de Bouillon, Crusader, King of Jerusalem (c.1060–1100)

'Trois gants', ubiquitous but ineffectual gendarme, real name Jules Antoine (1918–2003)

Marie Bodard, sweetshop owner (1903–89)

'Zizi', or 'Zizi Pan-Pan la Galette' (Louis Albert), Bouillon's

most libidinous man and a Bourland on his mother's side
(1934–2011)

Visitors, Tourists and Passers-through

Rimbaud, French poet and *Ardennais* (1854–91)
Verlaine, French poet and *Ardennais* (1844–96)
Baudelaire, French poet and reluctant traveller through
Belgium (1821–67)
Simone Signoret, actor (1921–85)
Gordon Jackson, actor (1923–90)
James Robertson Justice, actor (1905–70)
Jack Warner, actor (1895–1989)
Louis Jouvet, director (1887–1951)
Cardinal Mazarin (Giulio Mazzarino), Italian cardinal and
French statesman (1602–61)

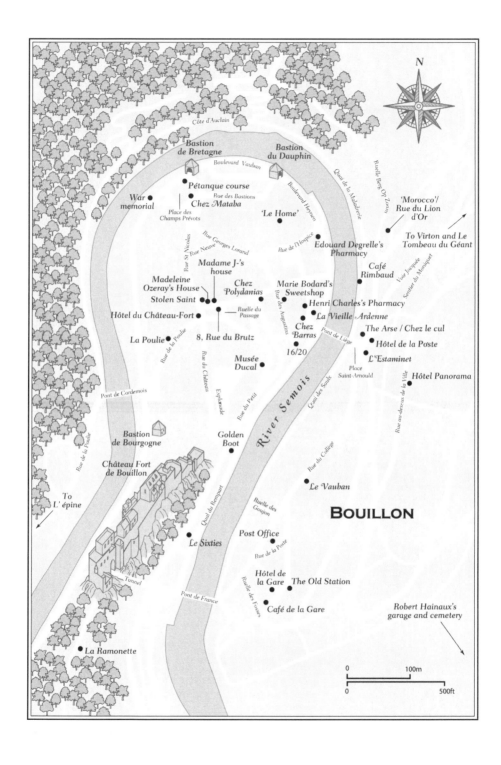

N

Côte d'Auclain

Bastion
de Bretagne

Bastion
du Dauphin

Boulevard Vauban

Boulevard Heynen

Quai de la Maladrerie

Ruelle Berg Or Zioun

Pétanque course

Rue des Bastions

Chez Mataba

War
memorial

Place des
Champs Prévots

'Le Home'

Rue de l'Hospice

'Morocco'/
Rue du Lion
d'Or

To Virton and Le
Tombeau du Géant

Rue Georges Lorand

Rue Neuve Georges Lorand

Rue St Nicolas

Edouard Degrelle's
Pharmacy

Café
Rimbaud

Voie Jacquée

Sentier du Moniquet

Madame J-'s
house

Madeleine
Ozeray's House

Chez
Polydanias

Marie Bodard's
Sweetshop

Rue des Augustins

Henri Charles's Pharmacy

Stolen Saint

Ruelle du
Passage

La Vieille Ardenne

Hôtel du Château-Fort

The Arse / Chez le cul

Chez
Barras

Pont de Liège

Hôtel de la Poste

La Poulie

Rue de la Poulie

8, Rue du Brutz

16/20

L'Estaminet

Place
Saint-Arnould

Hôtel Panorama

Musée
Ducal

Rue du Château

Esplanade

Rue du Petit

River Semois

Creu des Saulx

Rue au-dessus de la Ville

Pont de Cardemois

Rue de la Poulie

Bastion
de Bourgogne

Golden
Boot

Rue du Collège

Le Vauban

BOUILLON

Château Fort
de Bouillon

To
L'épine

Quai du Rempart

Ruelle des
Goujon

Post Office

Le Sixties

Rue de la Poste

Robert Hainaux's
garage and cemetery

Tunnel

Pont de France

Ruelle des Fosses

Hôtel de
la Gare

The Old Station

Café de la Gare

La Ramonette

0   100m

0   500ft

First there is memory, its sleights of mind;
then comes forgetting: the traitor betrayed.

DOORS AND WINDOWS OF WALLONIA

Before Television backlit them with its haunted blues,
its gauze of voice over voice, dubbings of *Dynasty* and
   Dallas,
there were firesides filtered through net curtains, shadows
pulling free from shadows. The furniture didn't furnish,
it loomed; heavy as cannon, it boomed darkness.

After closedown, after the trembling not-quite-stasis
of the *RTB* testcard, the blue glow lingered,
fizzed against mosquito nets, caught the flypaper garlands
with their incrustation of bluebottle and *mouche à merde*,
the banal shitfly with his coalface glitter.

That was the house's pulse, a comatose cellar-beat
to which my grandmother, Bouillon's only dressmaker,
pedalled kilometres of stitching, threaded her needles
seven to seven in daylight that took all day to die.
Her only books were swatches; she held them up

to the daughters and widows of Wallonia
fresh with their ideas from Brussels, of *haute couture*,
their cut-outs from *Paris-Match*: a small-town catwalk
of Deneuves along a corridor of Stockman mannequins
stuck with pins, stained with oil or grease, and for me then

(for me still) so oddly sexual with their tapered waists,
the perfection of their closedness. My face at the window, I'd watch
her busy sparrow-jerks inside the darkness that fleshed her out,
and smell the last-but-one all-day *pot-au-feu* that held its own
against the clashing scents of factory-owners' wives.

But the body that stayed caught in the full-length looking-glass
is mine, my drowning childhood pulling down, and these days
nothing – least of all my whole life – flashes by. Only the empty
mirror gives me back that time, and the lace curtains,
more air than lace, are sieves for shadows to pass through light.

Each time I breathe I breathe it in, that sublimate of all that's gone.
Essence of Indoors would be the perfume, if they made it.

MARIE BODARD'S SWEETSHOP

This small dark monochrome shop on a thin cobblestoned street with a pavement the width of a dustbin in the Belgian border town of Bouillon has become a legend in my children's bedtime. It feels more real to them than ever it felt to me, clouded over as it is in a mist of imperfect recollection and wishful thinking. Even at the time, when I was a child visiting it every day, I felt as if I was remembering it. Or that it was someone else's memory I was hosting, incubating it like a kind of surrogate. And as with so much of that childhood, I seem to remember not the things themselves but the memories of the things, as if the present I experienced them in was already slowing up and treacling over, fixing itself in a sepia wash. My children don't know that feeling yet, so telling them about Marie Bodard's sweetshop, filling it in, is like colouring in a black-and-white picture. Actually, since there were never really enough sweets to call it a sweet shop – 'magasin d'bonbons' described, in truth, its function rather than its essence – I find myself putting in most of the sweets too.

Like most shops and workplaces in Bouillon, it was really just someone's front room, where they sat, smoked and ate and watched TV, gliding around on fat felt slippers, and sold what they made or cooked, gutted, chopped or topped and tailed. The baker's across the road had their oven in the back of the house, their shop at the front. In the evenings they'd roll their sofa and armchairs in front of the bread-oven and gather around what was left of the day's heat. And it was a

particular kind of heat you got in the baker's in the evening: all residual, infiltrating the air rather than wrapping it in warmth, but always somehow enough.

The cafés and cigarette- and souvenir-shops were the same: a counter or a bar with the owner or landlord sitting on the customer side smoking, eating, reading the papers, until someone came in. At this point they would stop being a person living in their house and become a tradesperson or a shopkeeper – a *commerçant* – but only for the duration of the transaction. Even the butchers lived at the back of the shop, their immaculate living room flanked by a fridge room and a hoseable chopping room. (I always tried to pay the exact money, so as not to receive the bloody change, usually streaked with meaty pulp.) My grandmother, Lucie, also worked in the front room, using the corridor as a catwalk for her 'clientes' and a large cupboard built into the wall, whose door she had replaced with a thin curtain, as her dressing room. She over-worked and undercharged, cooked and kept house, did her own accounts and looked after her ailing husband, Eugène, my grandfather, damaged by a life in the factory owned by the people for whom Lucie made dresses.

Eugène ailed. For most of my childhood that seemed to be his job, his second career: to ail emphysemically, peeling potatoes and playing cards in the kitchen on a red formica table. He had been a useful local footballer for Le Standard de Bouillon, a mean *couyon*-player and local *pétanque* cham-pion, and in the days before the ailing began, it was my job to scour the cafés of Bouillon (about twenty for a population of two thousand) to bring him back for meals. Another habit of his, which runs in the family, was to piss outside wherever possible; indeed, to go out of his way to take a piss outdoors, even when he was comfortably settled indoors: even when watching television across the landing from the bathroom, he'd get off the sofa, go down the stairs, out into the *ruelle* and urinate against the outside wall. Sometimes he'd go up the small lane to the foot of the castle and piss against the rock, or down to the river, where he'd add a bladderful to the water he fished in. A piss was always a special occasion for men in the Lejeune household. Somewhere there is a photograph of three generations of Lejeunes – my uncle Jean-Pol, my son Osian and me – lined up at the water's edge pissing into it. The blur, the haunting at our shoulders, is Eugène, joining his progeny in adding his golden arc to the moving water of Time. And we in turn are paying what Robert Frost, in his poem 'West-Running Brook', called 'the tribute of the current to the source'. Eugène's nickname was Le Dènn, a *patois* corruption of the Walloon Le Djenn which is itself a corruption of Le gène, which is also the French for gene, as in progeny, genetics, genes, Genesis and eugenics. Eugène may not be where it all began, but it's his face we wear: my sister, my mother, my children and me.

When I'm asked about events in my childhood, about my childhood at all, I think mostly of rooms. I think of times as places, with walls and windows and doors. To remake that childhood (to remake myself) I'd need to build a house made of all the rooms in which the things and the nothings that went into me happened. And plenty of nothing happened too: it's The Great Indoors for me every time. This house of mine, this house of mind, would be like a sort of Rubik's cube, but without any single correct alignment or order: the rooms would be continuous, contiguous, they could be shuffled and moved about, so that its groundplan would be always changing. Just as they build for earthquakes or hurricanes, creating buildings that have some give in them, that can sway with the wind or sit on stilts in water and marshland, that can shake to their foundations but still absorb the movement, so the rooms in the house of a remembered childhood take on the shocks and aftershocks of adult life, those amnesiac ripples that spread their blankness along the past. Trying to remember is itself a shock, a kind of detonation in the shadows, like dropping a stone into the silt at the bottom of a pond: the water that had seemed clear is now turbid (that's the first time I've ever used that word) and enswirled.

One evening, my children asked for a picture of Marie Bodard's, so we set about recreating it. Remembering makes things real – it's the only guarantee that they've actually happened. Events owe their existence to memories more than memories owe their existence to events. Most of my childhood feels more real to me now than it did then. There's been a filtering out of overall meaning or point (half the time now I can't remember, if I ever knew, who most of the people in my mind's eye's memories are – they're like the forgotten cast of a lost film), and a heightening of detail: smell, taste, sight, touch. Textures and moods and states of mind or body (comfort, safety, warmth, or nausea, cold, sadness) push out the big things, the 'significance', the 'meaning' of the event. No, they don't push them out; rather, they become the means by which you get access once again to the big things. Death becomes concrete once more not because this or that loved family member or friend occupies your heart any more than they once did, but because the timbre of your sorrow comes back to you through your senses, through the feeling you had then, that day, which has stood suspended, has lived in its room unchanged, long after the house itself, the house that gave it context, has crumbled or been demolished. So the house of memory becomes a house in which all the rooms that have survived demolition have been arranged. The house has been flattened but somehow the rooms are all intact. I think that's what I mean.

LES VIEUX BOUILLONNAIS

My mother's family have lived in Bouillon for generations. Until the early twentieth century, many of the men worked as *miquelets*, small-scale loggers, cutting down trees in the forest that surrounds the town, chopping the wood and tying it up into rafts, and then floating them into Bouillon to be dried and sold. The attics and cellars of hundreds of Bouillon houses still store the old *miquelet* tools, and some *gîtes* display them on their walls to give their visitors that 'Ardenne profonde' feel. Later, like my grandfather's family, the men worked in one of the two factories, or, like my grandmother's, as domestic servants or hotel chambermaids, waiters, handymen or kitchen staff. As with many such families joined together by marriage, they all finished up living in the same place: 8 Rue du Brutz, a three-storeyed house made up of two houses knocked through. At the back of the house you can still see the outline of the badly filled-in front door of the second house beneath the oak beam that was its lintel. The steps that led to it are long-gone. On the other side of that infilling, the cavity that was once the doorway is now a cupboard full of sheets and bedding in the first-floor bedroom. As the closest bedroom to the bathroom and stairs, it was traditionally reserved for whoever was oldest or most infirm. In my time it was my great-grandmother's, then my grandfather's, and finally Lucie's, my grandmother's. I had it for a week myself when, aged about ten, I twisted my ankle by jumping from a high wall near the castle. Lucie, a dressmaker and seamstress, had made me a Spiderman costume after I had seen the film at René Lemaire's cinema. She must have forgotten to explain that the costume did not in itself confer the matching superpowers, because I embarked on a series of high-risk spider-stunts which finished with me being bandaged up and stuck upstairs for days, still wearing blue tights and red underpants, and watching Zorro, for which Lucie also made me a costume.

At one time there would have been more than a dozen people living in this house, spread across four generations, and since these were the days before retirement homes, many of the rooms lodged great-grandparents and grandparents from different branches of the family. Old ladies in colourful dresses could be found in the recesses of rooms you'd forgotten were there, like bright bobbins left in drawers. The house is now empty most of the year, and sits marinading in its past for nine months out of twelve. The people who lived and died there also marinaded in their pasts, and spent a great deal of time telling me their stories, or using me as an intermediary to tell themselves their stories. All of them had one thing in common: they thought they were the last of the *vieux Bouillonnais*.

KEYS

Watching an old police procedural, probably a Maigret, sometime in the early eighties while convalescing from glandular fever (an illness I experienced more as convalescence than as actual illness: I felt as if I was simply recovering from something, rather than actually having the something to recover from in the first place), it came to me: a thief pushing a key into putty so that its outline would be caught in the relief and he could copy it, then burgle the house.

That was memory, I realised: a putty with which you could make another key, which would open the same door, but never quite as well. In no time, you'd be burgling your own past with the slightly off-key key that always got you in though there was less and less to take.

COLLETTE

Collette was diabetic from the age of five or six. Her life was blighted by it. It made her erratic at work, ruined her diet, made her ill and undependable and depressed. It ruined her relationships and then her marriage. She was my aunt: tender, childish, loving, delicate and suicidal, my sister and I loved her, and loved the time we had with her so much it still hurts to call it back to mind. Besides, the more I think of her, the less there is, blanking over like a photograph left in the sun, so I have to be careful, ration out what is left of her because soon there will only be a whiteness in my memory, shaped to the outline of her going.

The only time Collette wasn't suicidal was when she had finally decided to commit suicide. I've seen it since, and I know now why so many people are surprised when someone kills themselves just when they seemed to have stopped being depressed, to have climbed out of the gulf and started once more to touch others.

It's the cliché of the left-behind. It always starts 'We all thought she had . . .' and 'he seemed himself again for the first time in X months or years', then peters out into the unsaid, the unsayable. Well, the reason he and she seemed, or looked or sounded well, good, better, was that they'd *decided*. That normality you thought you saw – the smiling again, the answering the phone, the coming to the door and waving you off like they used to – that was them making a last lap of the circuit.

I still have Collette's chess set, though the board is lost. As a child she wrote her name on everything, including the little box of chess pieces I am teaching my son to play with. So her name is everywhere, her old toys and books all signed, her school exercise books; even the wallpaper in her old room from when she was a child. And her suicide note. For years, and specifically from 1988 to 2004, it was kept in a drawer in the living-room cupboard with things like glue and scissors and Blu-tack, old spectacles, unpaid bills, stamps, sweets and loose change. It was the most visited drawer in the house – God knows why my grandmother put it there, where you would have to see it twice or three times a day. Perhaps it was her way of keeping it present, refusing to let go, but also trying to embed the terrible thing into routine, to dull it and wear it away with the quotidian, the way the sea works rocks into sand, so that it was no longer present as the catastrophe it was. Either way, it didn't work. 'A vous tous' said the envelope. I threw it out one day, suddenly angry at having spent so many years pushing it aside in my quest for this or that moment's object and never thinking to move it somewhere that was subject to less finger-traffic. Somewhere you'd actually have to *want* to see it before you did. But who would actually *want* to read a suicide note?

Actually, I did, sometimes, when I was drunk or depressed or feeling especially strong (in which case I might take it out and test myself, like a weight-lifter adding the extra weight-plates), I'd open it and take it in: its crisp practicality (allocation of objects, mainly), its blunt refusal to be in any way memorable, either in terms of phrasing or in terms of the quality or extremity of emotion it laid claim to. In the upstairs living room my grandmother had left Collette's hospital bag, her last hospital bag, because she had been to many hospitals, and that too had stayed for years, pitifully wedged between the arm and cushion of the sofa where it was dropped the day she died and they brought back her things. I threw that out too.

I did something similar when my grandmother died, and then my mother and then my father. Same house, different clearances.

MY SUITS

My last summer before going to boarding school – I was nine – my parents decided to save money on school uniforms by getting them all made by my grandmother. Like all home-made clothes, they were both better and worse: better cut, better material, but worse because it was being better that was the problem: my grey suit fitted me too well and looked too good. The last thing you want is to stand out sartorially, especially as a child, and especially in England.

As we neared the date I was due to leave, 1 October, leaving became real, more real in fact than when I really left, when I was too disorientated and sorrowful to take it in. I could taste the tears weeks before they came. I could already imagine myself gone, so that everywhere I went I could only think about what it would be like without me there. I was told this was just solipsism (though that wasn't the word they used), but really it was only sadness. Of course, when you try to imagine yourself somewhere you don't know and have never been, you can't do it – your mind slides off the surface of the images you conjure up like a finger on wet glass; can't get any sort of purchase. It's much easier to imagine the inverse: the place you know well without you. It hurts more that way around too, especially if you imagine the place you know without you while you're still there – you darken the edges of your own vision, put a black border around your days and they become like leaves curling inwards, dying from the outside in. Even as you live them forwards, you're looking at them from behind, seeing them as they would be if they were over. I spent most of my childhood with a foretaste of its pastness in my mouth.

So: I really was going – even in the slow, dilating time in which Bouillon seemed to exist, I was going.* *Look: the suit is taking shape*, I'd say to myself, watching it grow on the Stockman dummy as Lucie worked. The nearer it got to being finished, the closer I was to leaving; eventually it had legs and arms and was waiting for a body to fill it. It was not unlike watching your own coffin being made. That's how it felt: I over-dramatised it, of course, but over-dramatised is how I took it in: the fact of it *was* the drama, something the adults never admitted they understood. Adults pretended there was a fact, and then, orbiting that fact, ancillary to it and therefore wholly separable from it, was how you felt about it. 'Fais pas la comédie', they'd say: 'lay off the dramatics'.

* I think every child tries that experiment where, faced with a date in the future they dread, and believing the old adages about time going faster when you're busy or having fun, they slow down and avoid enjoying things too much, hoping to put the brakes on Time. This in turn means they don't enjoy the present, which gives them another thing, other than its pastness, to regret about the past.

LINING

Being measured for clothes, you learn a lot about lining. *Doublure* it's called in French, doubling. Linings played a big role in my childhood, as in all childhoods, along with an endless variation of lining-related associations: seams, hidden pockets, secret compartments, false bottoms, double folds. The lining was what you never saw but could always feel, a place of concealment, in-betweenness, a gulf between skins. All children are spies, double agents, *doublure* agents, but spies who have to make their own privacy since children are given no privacy, and they are forced towards the accoutrements of espionage. The lining, the *doublure*, is the most important of these.

Lucie was fond of linings. She claimed it was because of the cold, but her real reason was that she loved the craftedness of a good *doublure*; she liked the way, though people rarely saw it, a lining had to be as elegant and well made as the outside of the garment. Sometimes it could be spectacular, like someone's inner life: underneath the grey exterior the world sees, there would be a furnace of shot silk or a pool of seigneurial purple. The wearer might project the outer garment, but really their relationship was with the *doublure*. When the time came to discuss linings ('Et comme doublure, tu veux quoi?'), I would ask for extra pockets for pens or sweets or, later, for cigarettes.

She was fond too of turn-ups in trousers, which she claimed gave my school uniform a Cary Grant aspect. When

I was about fourteen I measured myself and sent her my details so she could make me a grey suit with turn-ups and baggy trousers and thin lapels, like the one I had seen in *North by Northwest*. I drew a picture of a suit and wrote down my inside and outside leg, arm, chest and waist measurements, and a few weeks later there arrived, in a brown parcel bound with string, a beautiful mid-grey suit with a silky mauve lining, that fitted perfectly and looked so good I wore it at weekends.

I think Lucie must have sewn a lining into time itself, because when I'm in her house I find myself feeling my way inside it for a whole life I hid there years before.

Cardinal Mazarin

'Monner un train Mazarin' – to flaunt yourself like Mazarin, to live the life of Riley – is one of those *patois* phrases I heard a lot. It goes back to the days when Cardinal Mazarin, Louis XIV's chief minister and successor to Richelieu, passed through Bouillon, leaving an impression of such wealth and opulence that the term is still used today. I first heard it when my grandmother used it to describe a neighbour buying a colour television. By the time she had her own colour television, she was using it to describe people who had two colour televisions. It's always someone else who flaunts themselves like Mazarin.

Trappist Beer

On one side is a bottle of Westmalle, on the other a bottle of Orval. Both are Trappist beers. Westmalle is made in the north, in the Flemish province of Antwerp, Orval here in the south, in the Ardennes, a few kilometres away from Bouillon. Both orders are Cistercian, though Westmalle is deemed a Flemish beer, and Orval a Walloon beer. Here in Belgium, even a Trappist must choose the language in which to keep silent.

THE ARSE

Monsieur Hanus (you don't pronounce the h, but you do the s, and with gusto too) ran a café off Place Saint-Arnould. No one can remember, if they ever knew, what his Christian name was: that's what having '(H)anus' as a surname does for you. By the traditional process of nickname-contagion his wife was known as 'l'Anuse'. 'Chez l'Anus', or 'Chez le cul', the café was called, and though it too had a perfectly good name of its own, no one ever invoked it. You couldn't blame them: both 'Hanus' and his café became known as 'Le cul', the arse, or, in *Wallon*, 'l'queu'. 'Dje vas tché l'queu', my grandfather would say ('Je vais chez le cul/ I'm off down The Arse') every Wednesday and Sunday night. My grandmother, who when she remembered thought herself a bit above speaking dialect, would say to me around ten or eleven o'clock: 'Descend un peu chez l'cul tu veux? Voir si l'Dènn y est': 'Pop down The Arse would you? See if Le Dènn's there'.

I'd walk down the Brutz and cross the pont de Liège (po' dî Lîdj) and find Eugène deep in a game of *couyon*, a complicated and specifically Walloon card game at which my grandfather excelled, and which he taught my mother, who carried its strange rules around the world with her long after she left Bouillon. I remember her trying to teach some diplomatic wives to play it in the British Embassy in Tehran, a few months before the overthrow of the Shah. Talk about a global village.

Eugène never liked leaving The Arse, though he was

always gentle with me, even when pretty drunk. I never knew how much he'd had, but his way of leaving the bench at which he'd been sitting was at once precarious and precise. He would turn shakily as he rose, take his backside off the chair, twist his shoulder and lean over and into the table, rise a little higher and take his body round so he was at right angles to the table edge, then at 180 degrees, with his back facing the table and still twisting and rising, so that by the time he faced the table once again he was fully standing up. It was as if he was unscrewing himself, and it chimed with the way he looked when he sat at his café table: screwed in, part of the fixtures and fittings. We'd then walk, him puffing and wheezing but holding my hand with a faltering grip, back to Lucie's icy welcome.

CORBION

Another of Eugène's regular cafés was 'Chez Mataba'. Mataba (someone else whose real name had dropped off) and his wife Germaine owned a small bar near the *pétanque* course, beside which was a blasted and derelict mini-golf course which seemed to have been modelled first on Chernobyl and then on the Chernobyl disaster. We played there while our parents and grandparents played *pétanque*. I remember the sound of the heavy metal *boules*, the muffled fine-gravel splash and the crisp clink of the balls as they nudged each other through what looked like a field of cat litter.

'Mataba' was so called because instead of saying 'mon tabac', my tobacco, he would say 'ma tabac'. He was from Corbion, a small town on the border with France, where they grew and dried tobacco and were reputed to be unable to gender their nouns. Verlaine and Rimbaud had a small cottage hideaway in Corbion which is now a ruin of slates and moss in a damp overgrowth of trees: the house was in Belgium, but the stream at the end of their garden was in France. There is a sign beside it – you can still see the layout of the cottage from the foundations – that says: 'Maison Verlaine. Ruines'. At one time, Corbion had several 'cultivateurs', who grew tobacco and dried it on wooden frames along the Semois. Old photographs show them drying the leaves, stiffening on wooden poles, dark and crumpled like dirty pillowcases and shot with nicotine-coloured veins. Some producers were moderately large businesses, others were single families, but it was a profitable living. 'Semois Tabac' cigars and pipe tobacco would be sold in Bouillon, and today only two producers still make it, mostly for the tourist market and mostly as a novelty. One of them now has a 'Musée du Tabac' adjacent to his business, and that says everything that needs to be said about the two-speed motion, the dual-tense, of economic decline: you commemorate what you are still doing until, little by little, doing it becomes itself the commemoration.

Bouillonnais, like everyone else, are adept at composing sweepingly universal rules from minuscule amounts of often unrepresentative data, and so 'Mataba' was held to be a typical Corbionnais because of his propensity for misgendering things. (My grandmother based her whole theory that people from Paliseul couldn't hack the cold on Mme Barras, the newsagent, whose catchphrase – 'Y fait pâââ t'chaud' – I still hear whenever her daughter sells me *La Meuse*). There was also 'Ma café', 'mon voiture', and, bizzarely, 'mon femme', though this might have been Mataba's deference to his wife's beefy masculinity. While it was true that Mataba did say these things, I've never heard anything from other Corbionnais to justify the extrapolation that it was a Corbion peculiarity. But to us, Mataba was a representative of his people, an ambassador for Corbion and its ways.

ROBERT HAINAUX

Robert Hainaux looked like a successful highwayman pretending to be an unsuccessful one. He ran the garage on the main road out of town, and was, despite his appearance, a rich man and a generous one. His garage was the second-last establishment in Bouillon as you left the town for France. The last establishment was the cemetery, where my and everyone else's family are buried: Eugène, Collette, Monique, and the rest of them, Elie and Julia and Lucie (my grandmother Lucie's spinster aunt, who apprenticed her as dressmaker) and Olga, Emile, Paul and Albert. That was always appropriate – with Robert's cars you were always, one way or another, one stop from the cemetery.

When I was a child and everyone drove drunk, when it seemed there was a minimum required limit of drink before you were even allowed to climb into a car (more if you were carrying passengers: it was a matter of conviviality), Hainaux drove around Bouillon in a series of battered Fiats, throwing sweets and coins out for children like a third-world dictator visiting a loyal shanty town. His yard looked like a rally-car graveyard, and his showroom was not much better. I never knew rust could come in so many shades and textures. These days it would be called a sculpture park and the arts-council funds would be running over it like rain in a poem by Verlaine (see below, 'Rimbaud and Verlaine').

Driving drunk was not difficult at Robert's garage, because he ran a café out of the same building. People picked up or dropped off their cars, or came to browse for new ones, and had a few glasses of beer or wine. The café was full of advertisements for those drinks that even then no one really drank, but which somehow define the sophistication of drinking: Mandarine Napoléon, Pisang, Maitrank, Dubonnet, Suze. There was a hypnotic one, for Byrrh, a neon outline from the fifties, which I loved to watch, of a glass filling up and being drained into the mouth of a red-dressed woman. The light would linger a few moments on the surface of the darkness before disappearing, and then the whole design would burst back out again. When it was off, the neon tubes looked dusty and rudimentary, and you could see the twists of wire that pinned the glass tube together; when lit, it was a spectacle.

Robert and his wife Paulette held their café ('Au point du jour') and lived above it with their grimy and feral Alsatians and their four children. Robert and Paulette had one glass eye each, having survived a terrible accident when they crashed their car into a deer on the road to France. She limped for the rest of her life, and he always contrived to wear his glass eye in such a way that it pointed upwards regardless of what the real eye was doing. It gave him the air of one of those saints in martyrdom scenes, his eyes aspiring heavenwards while the flesh accepted its mortification below. Robert looked like a saint in dirty overalls, still torn between higher and lower things and keeping an eye on both. Robert and Paulette kept chickens too, who would infiltrate themselves through the unclosed windows (not quite the same thing as open windows, which are a matter of agency and not forgetfulness) of their cars and lay their eggs. Goats roamed shakily over the carcasses of his decomposing Fiats as if crossing the steppes of some heat-beaten Greek island. We once hired a car from Robert which had several different kinds of animal shit scattered, pelleted or simply smeared around it. The only deposit Robert wanted for the lopsided eighties Fiat Ritmo was a kiss from Angharad, who wore his oily fingermarks on her white cheek for the rest of the day.

What made Hainaux the typical Bouillonnais, and typical too of a certain kind of life and culture, was that mix of industrial and rural that you get in small factory towns, or in places where heavy industry has been hewn out of nature. They're factory-glades amid the green. He was part of that movement from the soil to the assembly-line, except that there was no movement because the assembly-line came, then went, and the soil stayed. Like my grandfather and all those who worked in the factories in Bouillon and elsewhere, they had the habits of the country: they trapped animals and ate them, fished, kept chickens and pigs in their yards, and grew vegetables with a skill that was muted and bleak and uninterested in itself. (What would they think of today's self-conscious MILF, yummie-mummies and Nick Hornby dads tending their allotments in the mockneyfied suburbs of Euroland?)

They lived according to one set of rhythms – sun and moon, soil and seasons – but also clocked into and out of factories, did night shifts, manned machines and breathed in asbestos, coal dust, fumes. You see it across the world, and I've known those people in places as different, or differently the same, as Southern Belgium, Northern France, the South Wales mines or North Wales quarries; in my father's Northumberland and his father's Northern Ireland, but also in Greece, Romania, Spain, Italy. It's a universal specific, and it's the essence of Bouillon while at the same time being the essence of so many other places too.

I could feel nostalgic for it, because it's going, and it's going in a way that's wholly in keeping with the way it came: the factories are leaving, and though the soil still exists, no one really remembers it's there. Or not *as* soil anyway. The allotments are now wasteland or second homes; the work has moved or evaporated, and the forest is for walking, not trapping or fruit-picking or getting firewood. Actually, it isn't really for walking either – it's for watching tourists walk in. Robert's garage is finished and boarded up. 'Commerce à reprendre', says the sign, but none of his sons *reprised* it; they had neither his financial nous nor the chaotic and charming eccentricity that masked it. They feuded, lost money, then customers, then went to work for his rivals as mechanics: the new, smart Opel garage in Libramont industrial park, where the salesmen wear suits; the Renault garage near Bertrix, etc. My family has transferred its loyalty *en bloc* to the new Skoda garage in Noirefontaine, where the showroom windows are actually clean enough to see through.

Robert Hainaux died in 2007, and moved one space to the right: the cemetery. He took his brand loyalty with him to the grave, and was still advertising his cars from beyond it. The 'annonce' of his funeral in *La Meuse* newspaper went like this:

Le Petit Robert s'en est allé
pour enfin se reposer.
Fiat lux!

AESTHETICS

I've never known a people so able to shrug off the beauty of where they live as the Bouillonnais. Yet that too is a kind of universal. There are people who come here because it's beautiful, and those who stay here because they have no reason to go anywhere else. With the true Bouillonnais, a sense of the place's uniqueness goes so deep they don't let themselves notice it. But they know it – it's a certainty that so bypasses awareness that it can be mistaken for unawareness, even by the person inside whom the bypassing happens. This is because of some unconscious superstition that goes along these lines: if you notice it too much you turn it into something endangered. You look at the solidity of it all – the castle laid like a molar on its ridge of granite, the forest with its waves of green, the houses with their slate façades held together by a crumbling rust-coloured mortar I've seen nowhere else – and imagine that by thinking about it too much you're weakening it, sapping its foundations. Besides, it's also an effort to notice beauty all the time; it's too much like work, and this is Wallonia after all.

'FAIRE LE TOUR DE BOUILLON'

The Semois, a tributary of the Meuse, flows through Bouillon in the shape of an omega: it enters from the south, spreads out to take in streets and hotels, the shells of the two factories, a medieval castle, a handful of bakeries, butchers' shops, schools, two old people's homes and dozens of cafés, and then turns back and leaves town two hundred yards from where it came in. This slackness and circularity gives the Semois an especially meandering quality that suits the Bouillon temperament; as if it was not especially keen to reach its destination, and preferred to double back, take another look around, and generally play for time in liquid *flânerie*. 'Faire le tour de Bouillon' is what we say when we're going for an aimless walk, and this is exactly what the river does. On calm days, as you walk the riverbank, the water laps quaysides with the sound of a baby suckling at a breast. In the autumn, as the rains come after a dry summer, the parched banks of the Semois start to dissolve back into the silt they came from. The mud on the riverbank becomes lustrous and tender, the river rises and there's a brown translucent froth that trembles like a hem of dirty lace at the edges of the water. It's like looking through the window of an old house, trying to make out the slow, half-lit stirrings behind the pane.

TRIAGE

Angharad told me once, as I mooned about in the Bouillon house succumbing to a touch of the *ubi sunts*, to let go of the past. She's probably right. But really it's never been that simple, and I sometimes think it's getting worse, *this past business*, that it's rising up in me like damp creeping up a wall.

My parents travelled. They travelled light – by which I mean that their baggage was all internal – and had that peculiar ability to adjust that you find among maladjusted people. Off to school in England for three months at a time, I'd come back to the house, usually a different house each time (though it would still be called 'the' house, which fooled no one), and find my things gone. Usually I came back to a different country from the one I'd left. 'Why did you throw this out?', I'd ask about some shoes or a jacket or a few books I remembered and would have liked, if only for the purposes of orientation. 'You weren't using it', they'd reply. 'I wasn't using it because I was 3,000 miles away, in England, where you sent me to school'. But this was a mere detail. 'Mais quand même', said my mother. 'Well, still', repeated my father, before adding a flourish of *non sequitur*: 'fair's fair'. 'Il faut trier', my mother used to say, 'toujours trier'.

My parents had specific criteria when deciding whether to keep or throw out an object. If it could be drunk, eaten or smoked, it would be consumed or consume itself, and was out of the equation. Other objects needed to be affirmed on an almost daily basis or else they'd be under threat from the black bin bags: they had to be touched or applied or used. Sometimes it was enough to evoke them in conversation; a glancing reference from time to time might be enough to keep them from the articulated jaws of the bin lorry. My things and my sister's were never safe, because we were not there to vouch for their necessity. This must account for why we developed such detailed memories, such pain-inducingly precise recollections of tastes and smells and textures. And why, when, as a child in Iran, I won a used bicycle at a raffle (my number 13, which was my mother's lucky number too, came through), I wheeled it upstairs to my bedroom and slept with it leaning against my bed for a fortnight. The reason we liked Bouillon so much, and still do despite all the settling we've done (I think that's all we've ever done: settle) is that nothing got thrown away: last year's toys and the year before's had their place among Julia's and Lucie's and Eugène's things, and the things from the decades and even the century before. The Bouillon house is my Pharaoh's tomb, containing all the things I might need for another life, for the life I might have had in case it ever comes around again.

'Quand même'; 'fair's fair', etc. My parents often misused ready-made expressions not only in each other's languages but, by the end, in their own. By dint of all the travelling they did, and by dint of living with the other, each became gradually unmoored from their native tongues.

For the children, the commerce between French and English, with the added complication of Walloon-flecked *patois*, made for an exhilarating world of malapropism and cross-purposes. For example, I was once told, when I asked if I could stay up past 11 to watch a spaghetti western, 'you'll be lucky'. I took that to mean that I would in fact be lucky, and would, indeed, be able to watch my film. When I came down just before 11 in my pyjamas to watch it, I was given an explanation of the phrase which showed that if it meant anything it meant its opposite: that I wouldn't be lucky at all; that I would, in short, be unlucky. There are many things like this that coloured my childhood and made me feel as if I was always rubbing against English from the wrong side, that if translation was a tapestry, I was at the back with the hanging threads and dangling clutter of knots. In fact the tapestry was all back and no front, because I felt the same in French too.

Pissing in Your Chips

One of the most evocative confusions occurred with the passage
of my father's favourite expression – 'to piss in your chips' – into
French. For years I heard 'pisser dans ses frites' used about
people who had messed something up or rashly harmed their
chances of getting a job or earning some money, or snaring a
bride or a groom. In short, people who had shot themselves in
the foot. Since I had only ever heard it in French, I thought it
wasn't just a French term but a Belgian one; and not just a
Belgian one but a Bouillonnais one, part of the heritage *patois*
everyone trafficked in, and dovetailing very neatly with the town's
culinary landscape. If anyone, anywhere, was going to be pissing
in their chips, it would be us, here. I heard my grandparents,
aunts and uncles and even our neighbours use the expression,
until 'Pisser dans ses frites' belonged in my mind to Bouillonnais
and to Bouillonnais only. Only much later, testing it out on some
young *Arlonnaises* in my early teens, did I realise that the phrase
was in fact my father's exotic Geordie import that had grafted
itself onto the Bouillonnais branch and briefly flourished there
among people who took chips seriously and for whom the expression seemed so well designed that it was impossible to imagine
it being anything other than theirs. In truth, I had simply caught
it for the length of its brief life in our language, and though I
try sporadically to revive it in Bouillon or plant it further afield
in the French-speaking world, all the dictionaries assure me it
never existed. And yet . . . it seems an oversight here, in this
country whose great symbols are the Manneken Pis, the only

world tourist attraction that is smaller than most of the souvenirs that replicate it, and the 'baraque à frites', the chip stall. A combination of the two would surely become, in turn, the very symbol of national disaster. 'T'as b'en pissé dans tes frites là, vieux!': 'You've well and truly pissed in your chips there, mate!'

BOXES

The Italian dissident, Silvio Pellico, wrote a book called *My Prisons*; Verlaine wrote a memoir called *My Hospitals*; mine would be *My House Moves*; or maybe *My House Clearances*.

An old photograph of the four of us – Kevin, Monique, Sarah and Patrick – kneeling in front of another packing crate, heads bowed: are we packing or unpacking? Hard to tell, but either way we are at worship. The God of movement has his altars everywhere, and his altars are always portable.

CORRIDOR, 8 RUE DU BRUTZ

Coming here after a few months' absence, I find the air has thickened. It's like going underwater, and the water is always blood-temperature regardless of the weather outside. In this house the past is particulate; it's made up, as they call it in science, of 'respirable suspended particles', and you can feel them in your lungs and on your teeth as you enter the house.

However excited I am to come back – one phrase in French for returning to a place is *regagner*, to *win back*, and I enjoy the irony of that, because returning is always more about losing than winning – however excited I am to *win back* the place, I slow down as soon as I've opened the front door. It's out of respect for all that's settled, but also so as to miss nothing: the dust, the mould, the swell of wallpaper dampening in blisters, its tight little snarl as it lifts and curls where it meets the skirting board. It's like moving along the seabed, like being a diver: slow-footed, thick-limbed. I am diving, I know, but what am I finding? My anchor or my wreck?

CORRIDOR, 8 RUE DU BRUTZ II: THE CATWALK

Mme C— the factory owner's wife, proper in every way and with a patrician kindness my grandmother loved but my grandfather found insulting. 'Très correcte', Lucie would say admiringly, as Mme C— walked ('at least she does her own walking', Eugène used to say) back up to her eight-bedroomed house in its tight little acre of rose garden, overlooking river and forest, and facing away from the factory she owned. Looking at those bosses' houses, 'chez les patrons', I always thought they looked like averted faces, sitting on their hillsides with their biggest windows and doors facing beauty – nature, the greenery, the trout-torn, kayak-tormented Semois (as Yeats might have called it and Verlaine pretty much did) – and their backs giving onto the factory and shops and workers' houses. By the time I was a child, the factory had closed, but its shell was still there, and quite beautiful with its myriad windows catching the various gradations of sun. As the windows got broken, what started as a fanfare of red and gold squares became a few patternless clusters, then a handful of isolated pangs of light, then nothing. Now there is no factory either, just a grass-and-gravel landscaped garden with coach parking and bandstand, whose lack of character may have been easy enough to create but takes a lot to maintain: there isn't a day when the place isn't being weeded, pruned, mown or watered into municipal featurelessness.

I also remember, and more often, the clipped short steps

of long legs tightly pencil-skirted in. Here I could digress erotically for quite some time, because this was Mlle L—, who closed her eyes and imagined she was Catherine Deneuve, sashaying down the corridor in a catwalk daydream. I kept my eyes open. I didn't read *Madame Bovary* until I was eighteen, but Mlle L— exuded what I now know was Emma Bovarysm. She seemed to spend herself against her own dissatisfaction, but at the same time to define herself by it too, to need it. She sighed a lot and looked out of the window, its blocked infinities of lace. She'd put her hands on her taut hips, and imagine herself and her outfit, made by a small-town dressmaker for less than it would cost in a shop, in a place like Brussels or Paris, or, as we knew them then, 'even Brussels' and 'maybe even Paris' (see later: 'Even Brussels' and 'Maybe even Paris').

People from around the province came to Lucie with pictures of dresses and coats they'd cut out of fashion magazines, and Lucie would make them. I was amazed at the disproportion between work and worth: how could a person be cheaper to pay than a factory? And there was the irony that the very people who made their money and laid people off because machines could do the job were the same people who, when it came to their own things, wanted them made by people and not machines. Did I think that then? Certainly not, but now that I do think it, I realise I knew it long before I thought it.

Amid all this, there'd be the smell of food from the kitchen on the other side of the door, the smell of sleep from my grandfather, the steam from something boiling catching the windows and misting them up. It's all still happening, and

somewhere more real and tangible than just my memory. Do my children know this as they walk and play in the house, smelling the same smell, running the fingers of their minds along the inside of the house's *doublure*? And that smell, incidentally – it was always the product of what made it: the life, fast or slow, that animated it; the food they cooked, the things they brought in, the clothes they wore, the bodies washed and unwashed, old age, and that tamped-down off-sweet hesitant odour of someone you've never thought of as old but who now, suddenly, seems to have caught age itself on their skin. I remember that moment with each of them: Eugène already smelled old despite being only in his fifties, Julia was far into it; as for Lucie, I remember first smelling old age on her, and being made unsteady by it and perturbed, in about 1987, after Collette's death. I never smelled it on Collette or on my mother – there was no time. All those things have gone, and the people, but the smells are still there. It's all still going on, in the secret lining of time.

My children are playing along that corridor now. I can hear them from the room I'm writing in. Sometimes Mari tries on some oddities she's found and parades along the tiled floor with Eugène's walking stick and Lucie's spectacles, and it overlays the memory of the different *clientes* the way luggage labels overlay each other on steamer trunks: all there, all gone.

UNDERSTAIRS CUPBOARD

Walking sticks: 2.

Spectacles: 6 pairs.

Clogs: 5; 2 pairs, one odd.

Velvet bag containing funeral urn containing ashes (Kevin McGuinness): 1

Christmas decorations: many, in a box marked *Noël*, lying on a sharp sand of broken baubles.

Nativity Scene with missing pieces; all animals, no people: 1.

Carved elephant tusk depicting the corkscrewing hierarchy of a Congolese village, starting with assembled warriors and finishing with the chief: 1.

Ivory figurines, mounted on ebony bases: 3.

Various tins with old coins, thimbles, bobbins of thread.

Playmobil, in a box marked 'Klickys' (they are named onomatopeically here).

Cast-iron waffle-maker (*gaufrier*).

Lead soldiers with chipped paint and plaster cowboys and Indians.

Vintage diabetes kit, missing finger pricker.

School reports for Patrick and Sarah McGuinness from the early 1980s. In one of these, Patrick's physics teacher, Mr Pellereau, writes: 'he is such a nice boy that it is sometimes difficult to get angry with him'. 'Not a difficulty I've encountered much,' said my father when he read it. To have his ashes share a cupboard with those school reports he spent so long analysing is like burying a king with his favourite possessions.

Rimbaud and Verlaine

Verlaine on Bouillon:

> 'The Semois, lying dark on its bed of chattering stones,
> its trout (really I'd call them supernatural, and only my
> piety stops me calling them Divine), its castle, well . . .
> its *burg*, hewn out of granite among the endless woods
> . . . And did I mention the trout?'

Croquis de Belgique, 1895

Two famous *Ardennais*, Rimbaud and Verlaine, ripped their
soles in Bouillon and its environs, and would have been
knocking around town when my great-grandmother Julia was
a child. In fact, Julia and her mother worked as chambermaids in the Hôtel des Ardennes, one of the places where
Rimbaud and Verlaine lodged when they visited town, and
I can be reasonably sure that my great-great-grandmother
changed their sheets.

Rimbaud and Verlaine's story is a picaresque tale, not
just of drink, poetry, bohemianism and sexual dissidence, but
of a strange, elastic, attachment to place: a picaresque of
eternal return. We think of Rimbaud as the archetypal goer-
away. But he always came back – 'on ne part pas,' he said:
we never leave. So I imagine Julia with her parents, Lucie's
grandparents, the Bourlands and the Nicolas, catching sight
of them: Verlaine with his Mongol dome ('we instantly remark

the great asymmetry of the head, which Lombroso has pointed out among degenerates, and the Mongolian physiognomy indicated by the projecting cheek-bones, obliquely placed eyes, and thin beard . . .' – Max Nordau, *Degeneration*, 1891, pp. 119–20), and beside him a slut-faced adolescent boy he sometimes called his wife, walking without lifting his feet off the ground. They'd have smoked Semois tobacco in clay pipes, sampled the rain, inhaled the smell of still-to-stagnant water on a shallow bank, the heatwave bouquet of slowly poaching algae. Or, in the winter, the Semois lacquering the air, polishing it to a brassy, ringing cold.

Rimbaud was from Charleville, about thirty km over the border: 'Charlestown', he called it. Verlaine's father was from Paliseul, eight km from Bouillon, and his sister, Verlaine's aunt, helped bring up the boy. It was to her that he and Rimbaud often came to escape the police, or their creditors, or Verlaine's other wife, or just to hole up. Verlaine's aunt's house is still there, and a plaque marks it with touchingly feeble wording: 'Ici joua Paul Verlaine'. There's another important plaque, in Brussels, commemorating the occasion on which Verlaine shot Rimbaud in a hotel just off the Grand-Place on 10 July 1873. It is headed 'Il faut être absolument moderne', a quotation from Rimbaud's 'Une Saison en Enfer', and an ironic choice since the hotel 'A la Ville de Courtrai' where the shooting took place* was knocked down in the

---

* Just look at that: *Take* place. 'Take' place . . . It says it all, but only because place can't be *taken*. I cross-check it in French: 'avoir lieu', they say, as if a place could be had or held or owned. Even worse is the reflexive verb 'se passer': as if the passing was internal, as if time was inside the event rather than the event inside Time.

1960s to make room for this characterless modern block on which the poor plaque hangs. Unwittingly, it thus commemorates the destruction of places of memory, of *lieux de mémoire* in order for them to become, by dint of the plaque itself, *places of places of memory, lieux de lieux de mémoire*.

This is as it should be, because the best plaques are in any case the most tenuous. They assert the slimness of our hold on things, the delicacy of the relationship between the event, the time and place it happened, those it happened to, and those who remember it. Finally, they show us the gap between the event and itself. And what, anyway, is an event? Do they have plaques which say 'Here, between 19XX and 20XX, something slowly unfolded whose nature has not yet been established, which began long before then and somewhere else entirely, and will doubtless end that way too'? That's a plaque I would like to see. There's a trend in France these days for the humorous plaque: 'Ici, le 12 mai 1891, il ne s'est rien passé', which, beneath the joke, seems to me to answer to our deep and haunting need for some things, just a few times and places, to be free of meaning, unfreighted by any sort of significance.

'Ici joua Paul Verlaine'. 'Ici' . . . that's how the plaques begin: 'Here'. But after that they fall away into the amnesia and deliquescence they're designed to guard against. They are always made of something hard and durable too: iron, stone, slate. But it's the words on them, etched or in relief, chiselled

---

That line from Villiers de l'Isle-Adam's *Axël* that struck me when I first read it as chillingly beautiful: 'passant, tu es passé'. No wonder we invented something safe and abstract like 'to happen', which helps us avoid the time/place rub.

or enamelled, that lets them down. They look solid, but really they're melting as you read.

Belgium is a country of plaques. Everyone passed through, not many stayed. It's even truer here in Wallonia, the Belgium of Belgiums. So many plaques attest to a passing through, a temporary stay: 'Here' the metal intones boldly, assertively, 'Ici . . .'. Then the verbs come along and attenuate it, wear it away: so-and-so 'stayed', 'lodged', 'stopped' 'passed through' . . . so many verbs for transition momentarily stalled, Time's small speedbumps on the road out of town. In the Hôtel de la Poste in Bouillon (where my great-uncle Paul worked after the war – my grandmother's family were in what is now called the hospitality sector), a plaque reads that Napoleon III 'passa la nuit' there on the way to sign the Treaty of Sedan: a stopover between defeat and humiliation.

I remember in Sarajevo, InterRailing, finding the concrete cast of the feet of Gavrilo Princip in the pavement of the street where he shot Franz Ferdinand; there was of course a plaque too, but I remember thinking how unusual it was to see those feet: an actual imprint of people upon place, people upon time. As if everywhere we walked the ground was soft and yielding, every trace captured in the living clay, like the key in the putty. Princip's feet have been removed from the street they trod and put into a museum. They've also taken down the monument to him. Sarajevo was a town I already knew before I went, because it was caught for me in the line by Lawrence Durrell: a city 'composed around the echo of a pistol shot'. Why did I like that line so much? Because it primed me to experience Sarajevo as a kind of hologram: composed not around the bullet or the shot but around their echo, their resonating gone-ness. Their imprint, but their imprint on what? Composed around echoes: it's true not just about Sarajevo, but about everywhere I've been and ever returned to. The trace, the event long-spent, the words written in rain.

Verlaine was a connoisseur of rain, so many of his poems cocktail cabinets of different kinds of rainfall. Even his drink, absinthe, was the drink that needed water to flower into itself, ghost-grey. Verlaine and Rimbaud are still here: there is the Café Rimbaud on the riverside with its all-you-can-eat buffets, and, because what goes in must come out, there is D. Verlaine the plumber.

DEGRELLE

'I am Léon Degrelle and I was the Leader of Belgian Rexism before the Second World War. During the War I was the Commander of the Belgian Volunteers on the Eastern Front, and fought in the 28th Walloon Division of the Waffen SS. This will certainly not be regarded as a recommendation by everyone.'

This swaggering piece of understatement comes at the start of a letter written by Bouillon's most famous son (unless you count Godefroid the crusader, who probably never came here) to Pope John Paul II in 1979. It's the preamble to one of the most tasteless, glib and maliciously casual pieces of holocaust denial in the history of the genre, and was prompted by news of the Pope's imminent visit to Auschwitz in June that year. Degrelle is worried that the Pope's presence will legitimise what he calls the 'Hollywoodesque myth' of the Holocaust, and he even hazards a little joke about the Pope's own wartime incarceration: 'Some say you were yourself at Auschwitz; well then, you must have got out, since you are now Pope, and a Pope who, it seems, does not smell too much of Zyklon B!'

Degrelle was the Belgian Nazi leader, founder of the Rexist movement (a reactionary and militant Catholic group: 'Christus Rex') and leader of a collaborationist battalion, the Légion Wallonie, in which he served, first as a private and eventually as General, with such outstanding bravery that he became the German army's most decorated foreign soldier. The Légion Wallonie was incorporated into the Waffen SS after its heroic defence of the German army's retreat from Russia. 'If I had a son', he claimed Hitler told him, 'I would want him to be like you'. Degrelle lived until 1994, safe in exile in Spain, and to the end of his life he claimed that meeting Hitler was his proudest moment. 'Je suis plus Hitlérien que jamais,' he boasted in the 1980s: 'I'm more of a Hitlerite than ever.' Unlike many French and Belgian collaborators, who went along with the Germans out of pragmatism, weakness or fatalism, or saw collaboration as an acceptable price to pay for the establishment of an authoritarian, Catholic and monarchist national order, Degrelle was a thoroughgoing and extravagantly committed Nazi who never expressed the slightest regret for his actions nor sought to invoke any kind of exculpatory contexts for them. He welcomed the Nazis as soon as they invaded, and was finishing his articles with 'Heil Hitler' within days of the German occupation. Even in December 1944, during the Ardennes offensive, as the Allies advanced and the game was up, he fought the liberation of Belgium and killed his own countrymen with an exultant devotion to Hitler and Nazism.

Degrelle claimed that the Walloons were a lost Germanic tribe that was destined to rejoin the greater Reich. The idea of the Walloons, with their instinctive aversion to anything that smacks too much of work, as being related to the Germans, would have baffled anyone it didn't amuse. Try telling that to Paprika, Bouillon's laziest man, who held a party to celebrate sixty years on the dole, and managed to get the council to fund it as a piece of 'folkloric' spectacle (I'm not sure this is true – it may be a legend created to convey a reality by inventing it). I once ran the lost Teutonic tribe theory past my grandmother, who for a moment forgot herself and told me 'Tê ch'teu' ('Tais-toi') – this was before I knew that she and Eugène had the house expropriated by the Germans and were sent to pull up vegetables in Vichy France for most of the war. I still have a German helmet which I found in the cellar when I was clearing it out. So whenever I imagine the house as ours, I have to, as the phrase goes, 'factor in' its occupation by German officers. But I can't sense it the way I can sense the other things that happened here – there are no traces, and I can't even introduce them into my fictional memories of the house, into my idea of what the house remembers about itself. Maybe a plaque would do it.

Degrelle escaped capture, was sentenced to death *in absentia*, lived out the next sixty years in Malaga, enjoyed nearly six decades of insolently good health, and made no attempt to hide or go underground. He worked as an occasional consultant for General Franco's security services, and his company was involved in the building of US military bases in Spain. There was something of the pantomime Nazi about Degrelle, who never missed a chance to pose in his SS uniform or wear his Iron Cross and his Order of the Oak Leaf, and he was often photographed in front of Nazi flags and other paraphernalia. He remained to the end a vocal neo-Nazi, anti-Semite and dubious friend to the stars. There's a comical photograph of him, 'avec son ami Alain Delon', during the filming of *Zorro* in Spain in 1974. This was the same film of Zorro I watched with my great-grandmother, who had known Degrelle, in her room when I was a child. Delon is in his Zorro uniform, and Degrelle is in a crisp cream suit. He married off his daughters in full SS regalia and stooping under the weight of his Nazi decorations. He once sent some of his cartoons to Hergé, and later claimed to have been the inspiration for Tintin. Is it true? We do know that in the 1930s Degrelle was in the US working as a correspondent for *Le Soir* when Hergé was a reporter at its Brussels office; we know that they knew each other, and we know that Degrelle sent Hergé some American comics, which according to Degrelle, set Hergé off. What is for sure is that Degrelle has a small place in the grey area that is Hergé's own relationship with the German occupiers.

Fabulist, liar, vainglorious fantasist, fascist dandy, what strikes us the most about Degrelle in the recordings we have of him is his complete undefeatedness. On recordings you can find on YouTube, he rails in a thick Bouillonnais accent (sixty years since he visited the place but it's as if the accent has been kept in brine, perfectly preserved) about world Jewry, Bolshevism, Islam, and talks about his friends Jean-Marie Le Pen, Franco, Salazar, *et al*. Another of his visitors was the French actress Arletty who was herself arrested after the war for her relationship with a German officer. Her reply – 'Mon coeur est français mais mon cul est international,' 'My heart is French but my arse is international' – shows that a certain panache is always useful, even at times of vigorous national retribution. Degrelle's family paid the price: his brother, a local pharmacist, was assassinated by the Belgian resistance (see below, 'Edmond Degrelle and Henri Charles'), and his mother died in prison after the war.

Degrelle himself died a defiant, happy, tanned, unapologetic Nazi, and asked to have his ashes scattered over the 'Tombeau du Géant', a beautiful hill beside Bouillon covered in pines and encircled by a bracelet of water that doesn't just run over the stones but flexes like clear muscle over its riverbed. It's a Wagnerian location, a giant's tomb in the Ardennes, and it says something about the way Degrelle saw himself: consumed in a Walloon *Götterdämmerung*. In the end a group of neo-Nazis accompanied one of Degrelle's comrades-in-arms to Germany, where they clandestinely scattered his ashes on the site of Berchtesgaden. A final, filial, homage to the Führer, these Bouillonnais ashes invested in German soil.

There is no plaque or monument to Degrelle, but he is the cause of plaques and monuments to others. To this day, the grave of Degrelle's youngest brother, who died at the age of two, is still tended and flowered, by persons unknown, in the infant's section of Bouillon cemetery.

WALLOON PARTY SONGS

Walloon is a variety of French dialect, and was until recently one of the few minority languages still spoken in the cities and industrial heartlands. This can be inferred by the preponderance of aprons and overalls on the record sleeve of this old family favourite. Walloon is concentrated around the big cities of Liège, or Lîdje, and Charleroi, or Tchârlerwé, where the legendary Bob Deschamps came from. Although Walloon has declined as a community language, its riches still seep into Belgian French and, notably, into the various *patois* of towns like Bouillon. In fact, Bouillon *patois* sounds so much like Walloon that you have to know Walloon in order to know that it isn't. The only other country where Walloon was spoken in any concentration for the duration of more than one immigrant generation is Wisconsin, where thousands of Walloon industrial workers went to live in the mid-1800s. Recordings from the Wisconsin Oral History Network show that a surprising number of people still spoke Walloon into the 1980s. The number is surprising not because it is large, but because it is any sort of number at all.

Edouard Degrelle and Henri Charles

Degrelle's story is intertwined with Bouillon's and thus, in a small way, with my family's.

Degrelle had a brother, Edouard, who ran a pharmacy on Boulevard Heynen. When I was growing up the building was a Tiercé, the local betting shop, and was flanked by a *friture* and a grocer's, and sat among a few chokingly drab clothes shops. There's now an artisan-*glacier* and a chocolate shop, and several of the old shops have become private homes. They've kept their huge windows but these are blocked off with thick lace curtains, through which you can still make out the blue of TV screens and old people moving with the slowness of fish in an aquarium. Across the river you can see the pedalo-hire kiosk and the Café Rimbaud.

My grandparents remembered Edouard Degrelle as a harmless if unendearing man. He was also a member of one of the two local football teams, the Saint-Louis de Bouillon (my grandfather played for the other one, Le Standard), and despite his brother's ugly notoriety he managed to live a relatively normal life in the town. Opinion on him is divided. To some, like my grandparents, he was withdrawn, not overtly political and certainly not a collaborator of the same stripe as his brother. For others, he was a 'Rexiste ardent' who propagandised for the Germans. This claim is not sustained by the living memory of any of the people who recalled him and to whom I have spoken over the years, and there is no evidence for it in any documents, letters or reports of the time. But Edouard Degrelle needed to be depicted as a Rexist *collabo* by both sides: by those who killed him, in order to justify their action and its terrible consequences, and by the Rexists and pro-Nazi collaborators, in order to create a martyr and justify their reprisals. These reprisals were ordered by Léon Degrelle, and were so vicious even the local German SS chief balked at carrying them out and complained about Degrelle to his superiors. Edouard Degrelle's life must be worth a novel; there must be enough innocence, guilt, mixedness of motive, ambiguity and ill-luck to make it, in its way, a micro-history of twentieth-century Europe. There's a poignant extra detail about Edouard Degrelle, which is that he was named after a sibling who died aged two and is now buried in Bouillon cemetery (see 'Degrelle', above). Various bottles and phials with Pharmacie Degrelle labels can still be found in *brocantes* and car boot sales around Bouillon, and in the cellar of 8 Rue du Brutz.

The Belgian resistance had failed to assassinate Léon Degrelle at least twice. He was too well protected, and they lacked the manpower or the intelligence. An easier target was his brother, whose misfortune was simply to be related to the wrong man at the wrong time. At around 17.00 on 8 July 1944, as Edouard finished work, he was gunned down by four members of the 'armée secrète'. To this day no one knows who killed him, though the organisers are alleged to have been Bouillonnais and the killers *maquisards* from elsewhere, perhaps from across the border in France. Degrelle's response: 'Bouillon doesn't know what it's let itself in for: the town will weep tears of blood, blood will flow. I will avenge the death of my brother and the wrongs done to my father ten years ago.' Degrelle was in a mood to settle scores, and many of the hostages he ordered taken were simply people he didn't like or who had offended him, often in quite banal ways, over the years. The Germans talked him down from his original 100 hostages to be executed to 46, who were taken to Arlon prison and were lucky enough to stay there, unexecuted, until the end of the war. After the first spate of hostage-taking, Degrelle decided to add three personal enemies to the list, but have them executed separately: Louis Bodard, a Catholic activist and former friend of the Degrelle family who rejected Rexism and campaigned against it; René Pierlot, engineer in the *ferronnerie* factory where my grandfather worked; and Henri Bodard, whose daughter, Mme Clément, founded the museum of Bouillon and for whom, in the 1990s, I wrote and recorded the English-language guided tour of the museum (it's still my voice you'll hear on the headphones*). Henri Bodard, a civil servant and brother of Louis, was accused of perhaps the noblest-sounding crime, and certainly the most typically Walloon: 'administrative sabotage' – slowness and inertia in the fulfilment of orders, lack of urgency at work, and the general obstruction of office business. All three were executed on 21 July 1944 on the outskirts of Bouillon. A small tatty memorial, more like a roadsign than a monument, marks the place where the Gestapo shot them. André Millard, one

* When I last went to the museum, in 1993, I took with me a girl I was trying to impress and boasted to her that it was I who was giving the guided commentary. She began laughing as soon as she donned the headphones. This was because, through some technical hitch that has still not been righted, the tape plays at one-and-a-half times normal speed, and the result is that I sound like a breathlessly excited Charles Hawtree.

of the surviving hostages recently honoured by the town, had been arrested by the Gestapo for no other reason than that he had been seen by an informer arguing with Edouard Degrelle outside his pharmacy. It was assumed therefore that Millard had had something to do with the murder. Millard maintains that their argument was about stamp collecting, that Millard, then in his late teens, had refused to swap a particular stamp with the Rexist leader's brother. The mix of quotidian banality and mortal terror in which Millard and so many others lived is a facet of life under the Occupation.

Forty-eight hours after Edouard Degrelle's murder, a group of Rexist killers came to Bouillon from Brussels and shot Henri Charles, the town's other pharmacist, in his shop on the Grand' Rue. That murder too was ordered by Degrelle, and one thing that strikes me about the way Degrelle operated here is that it reveals the essence of the reprisal mentality: on the one hand it must be (that word again) *disproportionate*, as in 100 executions for one murder; on the other hand it must also have a sense of symmetry, as in one pharmacist for one pharmacist. There's now a plaque where Henri Charles was killed, and the shop is now a beer supermarket and successful microbrewery, 'Le Marché de Nathalie'. Their best-selling beer is the Cuvée Godefroid, a blonde ale with a label that depicts a scantily-clad voluptuous crusader's woman, or perhaps a crusaderess in her own right, with tight comic-strip buttocks and an armoured bikini. She rests her hands on the hilt of a huge sword and her eyes on the imposing mass of Bouillon castle. Bouillon was without a pharmacy for the remainder of the war. When I was a child the building was a small cooperative supermarket, the Épécé, which closed in the late eighties. Bouillon had two other supermarkets, and all of them have closed, to make way for the excellent Colruyt, a great hangar of a place where one of Philippe Albert's brothers works (see 'The Golden Boot').

At its peak, Rex had over 700 votes in the Bouillon area, though this is a touchy subject. Part of the problem with Rex was that, before the war, it was a popular and radical conservative movement that claimed to defend workers and small businesses from what Degrelle called 'Banksters', a term for rapacious gangster high finance that would strike a chord today. It was after the war that it became allied to the German cause, through Degrelle's Führer-adulation ('Degrelle ou la Führer de vivre' is the tongue-in-cheek title of a documentary about him), and lost much of its support, though Degrelle filled the ranks of his Légion Wallonie with people from the area. When I was growing up, Bouillon was visited sporadically by TV crews and journalists making programmes or writing articles about Degrelle, or the war, or Belgian collaboration, and people stayed tight-lipped. Old people never liked to talk about Degrelle, because they understood something that we didn't, namely that for a civil society to function the right kind of forgetting is just as good as the right kind of remembering, and certainly better than the wrong kind.

The owner of the 'Vieille Ardenne', whose daughter I spent time with as a teenager, gets it about right when, in a *vox pop* for *Le Soir* about Degrelle, he reminds us that Bouillon hasn't produced many famous people, and apart from Godefroid and Degrelle none of its children have ever really made it on the outside. There's a nuance of pride when he mentions them together. He then adds, provocatively, 'The one was no better than the other'.

'Discuss,' you want to say, 'discuss'.

CRIME WAVE

In sitcoms, when someone takes an unnecessary precaution, they are challenged: 'where d'you think this is – the Bronx?' Here in Bouillon, 'the Bronx' is replaced by 'Virton', a town of 11,000 inhabitants forty-two km away. Try it: 'Where d'you think this is? Virton?'

In the early nineties my grandmother read in the local paper that an old lady in Virton was robbed by an intruder while she sat dozing in her living-room. This crime captured Lucie's imagination. With all the dozing she did in her own living-room, that old lady could easily have been her. One day when I returned to Bouillon for a holiday I found the front door locked. This was a first. I was in my twenties, and I saw this as another broken link on the chain of my childhood. Christ, I didn't even know that door *had* a key. (I have it now, use it quite often, and know its reluctant grincing sound as it turns.) I went round the back, through the alleyway, and in through the kitchen, which was open. There was Lucie in her Voltaire armchair watching TV. But something had changed.

For Lucie, who had been through many bereavements and privations, this remained the worst thing that could happen: to be burgled in your own home. And it hadn't happened halfway across the world, but in Virton. After that, for years to come, or for the few that remained, she would invoke the Virton story: she began locking the doors when she went out, or went to bed. If she was in the front room, her old workshop, she'd lock the back door; if she was in the back watching TV, she'd lock the front. 'You know what happened in Virton don't you.'

The coda to the Virton story is that the old lady who was the victim of the burglary was a little confused, mid-doze, and had forgotten that the intruder was in fact her grandson, who had popped in, as he regularly did, to get some money to do her shopping. Afraid to wake her, the only stealing he did was in and out of the house. In the throes of a senior moment, the *Virtonnaise* saw what she took to be a stranger in the penumbra of her living-room, and called the police, who responded with Walloon urgency eighty minutes later. One of the officers was able to establish the nature of her confusion when the boy returned with two shopping bags and her change.

My grandmother read this story in *La Meuse* (Province of Luxembourg edition) and knew how it ended. But she focused entirely on the intrusion and ignored the happy conclusion. After that, Virton, the name alone, was enough: a shudder, a quick tour of the doors and windows, double-checking she had double-locked them.

Newshound

La Meuse is the regional newspaper, slack with news from all over Wallonia. It has local supplements, and ours, for the Ardennes, proves there is no such thing as no news. Slow news maybe, but never no news. 'It is a rich world, full of minor deeds', writes William Bronk in his poem 'The Rain of Small Occurrences', and if I ever doubted him, *La Meuse* is there to set me straight. This summer, these minor deeds were a welcome relief from what we Belgians (there's a phrase we Belgians don't use much) still call, more from habit than engagement, *national* news: the constant threats of divorce between Flanders and Wallonia that would make any real divorce, were it to happen, feel like a mere tautology.

My uncle Jean-Pol – aka 'Johnny'– Lejeune was, to all intents and purposes, the sixties in Bouillon.* Suspected of

---

* Johnny introduced himself to an American friend visiting Bouillon as 'Johnny Lejeune: Leader of a Generation', and claimed that the café on the Ramparts called 'Le Sixties' was named after him. I once took a rather proper girlfriend from Luxemburg to visit Johnny and Marie-Paule in their house in Martelange, a town that straddles the Belgium/Luxemburg border so completely that one side of the main street is Belgian and the other Luxemburgish. When Johnny had fed us and declared himself too drunk to drive us back across the border, he showed us to our guest room and told us to leave the door open if we intended to have sex: 'j'aime encore regarder', he said, 'I still like watching'. He then remarked on the similarity – in looks, voice

being a delinquent, he became one. His behavioural problems were made worse by the beatings he received from his teachers for being left-handed. It was an attempt to turn him into a right-hander, and this, 'la main du diable' as they called it, was something even the secular school punished with a cultish superstitiousness. His left hand bled and they beat the skin off his knuckles. He never became right-handed, but he did become very angry, and to this day has an anti-clericalism that would make Dawkins blench. It's a particular kind of atheism, one where you can't actually let go of God, because if he were not there it would be impossible to insult him. It's a facet of life in Catholic societies. You can't rebel against intelligent design, or the selfish gene, or even evolution. But you can rebel against God. In terms of pure 'révolte', it's very good value, because you get several targets for the price of one: your parents, your school, your country, and, if you play it right, yourself. And that's just for starters. After that there's architecture, a lot of art and literature, plenty of music and a raft of Judeo-Christian values, all at no extra cost. Science doesn't have a hope in hell against that package, which is why so many atheists still plump for God. 'The last judgement', Johnny used to say at mealtimes as my great-grandmother tried to say Grace, 'it's God who'll have to answer for himself': 'c'est Lui qui aura des comptes à rendre'.

Johnny is now a journalist for *La Meuse*, and one of their Ardennes correspondents. 'Hang-glider makes emergency landing – more through prudence than danger,' is one of his front-page headlines. 'Un *scoop*', he tells me over his morning

---

and deportment – between my girlfriend and Lady Penelope, the Thunderbirds puppet, and called it a night.

glass of Luxemburgish Pinot Gris : 'I was first on the scene, and I had my camera'. We are in the Café Op de Trap, just across the border into the Duchy of Luxemburg where the drink is cheaper. The accompanying photo, which Johnny took, shows an unscathed man walking away from an accident that never happened. There's no such thing as no news.

The big summer story in these parts, apart from the inconclusive disintegration of the country, concerned the late Alain Garbar, 51, of Montigny-le-Tilleul, who attempted suicide by sitting beside a large butane gas bottle and lighting it with what he hoped would be his last cigarette. He destroyed his house and the houses of his neighbours on either side, and injured himself terribly, while contriving to remain alive. 'What kind of a country is this, where you can't die in peace', he asked the paramedics who brought out his badly burned body. A week or so later he died of his injuries, by which time M. Garbar was merely an inset on page 4 with no picture.

Because of the time-lag between his death and the action that led to it, I can't write that he 'committed suicide'. Even in the crude causality of self-harm, it's difficult to express this species of temporal filler that seems to have been injected into the join between what M. Garbar did and the result of what he did. Instead I have to write 'attempted suicide' and then add, further along the story, the rider that he did so 'successfully'. But do I mean 'successfully'? What I mean, surely, is that he died as a result of an unsuccessful suicide attempt, which is an absurd statement.

ALL PHOTOGRAPHY IS TRICK PHOTOGRAPHY

One morning I find Osian sitting at the table with a box of old photos. He looks like he is playing solitaire. The box is one of those big but shallow cardboard boxes Lucie received her cloth in, and he is sorting them according to resemblance, guessing who is who, who might be related to who. He's pretty good at it – children have a way of knowing while not knowing about their ancestors. He calls himself 'Osian Lejeune' here, which makes me happy, and he imagines what it would have been like if Guy rather than my mother had 'married English' (as they call it) and left the country. If I, his father, were the local politician, deputy Mayor of Bouillon and regional arts minister, and my cousin Patrick had been the lecturer in a British university. If he were at the *école communale* that his grandmother attended and his great-aunt taught at, and if Alexandre, his cousin, were at Ysgol y Gelli in Caernarfon. The photographs help with these imaginings, each one like a door into a house, and the people in them stand or sit as if they were welcoming you into room after room. A box of photographs is all rooms and no house.

What throws him about these photos, and it threw me when I was his age, is that the box doesn't just contain pictures of our family, people we see now on the street twenty, thirty or even eighty years older, but photographs of Lucie's best dresses with strangers inside them. That was how she recorded her creations: interspersing family and friends with dresses

she had made. Thus we have the Bouillonnais, roughly clothed or, when well-dressed, bearing that stamp of discomfort you see in people in their Sunday best, their 'trente et uns'. With men, it's an itching around the neck, the tight collar, the pendulous slack tie with the fat-fingered knot. With women it's the stiffness, the fear of making creases in the dress. Then we find sparkling brides snapped by society photographers, a retinue of factory owners' wives and daughters at millionaire banquets that are always held in pavilions and banqueting halls in Namur or even – *even* – Brussels. There's one in a hunting lodge done up to look like the Congo. For years I thought it was the Congo, but there are no black faces, so perhaps it was some industrialist's themed Africa room, full of ivory, palms, and elephant's-foot plant pots. Osian is sorting them, asking me who was who, who is still who. He puts them together in pairs, then threes and fours. Chasing the gene, chasing Eugène, who he finds in a photo of the football club, Le Standard de Bouillon, and again in a dark photograph holding my mother on Cordemois bridge.

Osian says it's like playing 'Happy Families'. I feel on safer ground calling it 'Pelmanism'.

EVEN BRUSSELS . . .

I used to think Evenbrussels was a place: 'Mêmebruxelles'. That's how I first heard of the capital city: prefaced always by the word 'même'. Success of any kind has its staging posts, and for us it was: Arlon, Namur, Mêmebruxelles. As in: Lucie's dresses are worn in Arlon, Namur and *even* Brussels.

PENSION CALENDAR

Mme J— lived across the road from my grandmother on Rue du Brutz. This photograph, taken in 2010, is of the calendar as it hung the day they took her away to the old people's home, 18 September 1994, where she died a short time later. There's something about old people in their own homes: they can live in them for years without quite managing: managing the cooking, the stairs, the washing, the laundry, the bills, the heating, the water, the personal hygiene and the TV remote control. When I say 'not quite managing' I mean, basically: managing. In a similar way, when I said 'managing' I'd in fact mean 'not quite managing'. My point is that that definition of 'managing' needs to be as flexible and blurred as possible, to allow the old person who is managing/not quite managing maximum leeway to stay in their own home. Why?

Because suddenly, when their children or grandchildren decide it's time to move them to an old people's home where these things will all be managed for them, they decline fast or die, or decline fast *and* die – either just before going into the home (as my grandmother did: heart attack on the stairs on the way to the bathroom the day before they were due to take her to see the home) or just after reaching the home, as Mme J— did. These places used to be called 'Maisons de retraite'. Now they're just called 'Un Home', as in: 'il est temps qu'elle aille dans un home': 'it's time for her to go to a home'. 'Le Parking', 'Le Traffic', now 'Le Home'. My consolation is that my grandmother never knew enough English to feel the

painful irony of that foreign word 'home' being used to desig-
nate the place that would have dislodged her from hers.
Generational repotting takes you from home to 'Un Home'.

Mme J—'s house hasn't changed since she left, as the
descendants can't decide whether or not to sell, though it still
gets cleaned twice a month. Just above the date in the picture
below is a calendar from the post office showing on what days
of the month to collect your pension. It reads, in blunt
bureaucratese, 'Mariés', 'Isolés', 'Veufs/Veuves'. It's hard not
to read it also as the order in which things happen: first
marriage, then isolation, and finally widowhood. I've shuffled
them around a few times and decided that any other order
would still be preferable to that one.

1086 (F)

Au cours de cette année, votre pension de retraite vous sera payée aux dates reprises dans la colonne marquée d'une croix (X).

MOIS – 1994	MARES			ISOLES			VEUFS VEUVES		
JANVIER	7	10	11	17	18	19	21	24	25
FEVRIER	7	8	9	15	16	17	21	22	23
MARS	7	8	9	15	16	17	21	22	23
AVRIL	7	8	11	15	18	19	21	22	25
MAI	9	10	11	16	17	18	24	25	26
JUIN	7	8	9	15	16	17	21	22	23
JUILLET	7	8	11	15	18	19	25	26	27
AOUT	8	9	10	16	17	18	22	23	24
SEPTEMBRE	7	8	9	15	16	17	21	22	23
OCTOBRE	7	10	11	17	18	19	21	24	25
NOVEMBRE	7	8	9	15	16	17	21	22	23
DECEMBRE	7	8	9	15	16	19	21	22	23

SEPTEMBRE

1994

18

DIMANCHE

Quai du Rempart 11 B

16/20

After the war, some parts of Bouillon that had been destroyed were not rebuilt. On this beam you can see the old house number ghosting the new one that unemphatically overwrites it: somewhere along this street one or more houses have gone missing.

Sixteen or twenty? As it stands it's a perfect example of the kind of double vision of past and present I get as I walk around here: two tenses wrestling slowly while the rust closes over them.

LE DÈNN

Another legend in my children's bedtime is their great-grandfather Eugène's temper, which I greatly exaggerate for disciplinary purposes. In order to evoke his voice for them – it's hard, he was very quiet, there are no recordings of him in my head, but of his heavy slow breathing, yes, the lungs emptying, wheezing like an old accordion – I play them a CD of the French singer Jacques Marchais belting out 'L'bon dieu dans la merde', a great anarchist anthem of the 1890s.

The voice is a snarl, 'embedded', as Mike Davis says about anarchism, 'in decadal cycles of class struggle and repression, and in cultures of plebeian anger'. Children don't know about that, but something of its truth reaches them in their inquisitive minds. They know that my grandfather worked and died from work. They don't yet know what collective grievance is, but they are wise to something about it, even if they don't know that Eugène ruined his lungs working in a factory which then laid him off early and under-pensioned. They know that he lived at home but not that he lived essentially off his wife's job, which was skilled work, but also work that, as he saw it, came from luxury and excess, not to mention from the disposable income of the very people who had disposed of his time, his health and eventually him. *Disposer de*: to dispose of in the sense of have at one's disposal, and to dispose of in the sense of cast off, throw out, chuck away.

Anyway, 'L'bon dieu dans la merde' is delivered in a great

rich truculent snarl, and when the children hear it they're consumed with excitement and a kind of awe:

Si tu veux être heureux, Nom de dieu!
Pends ton propriétaire,
Coup' les curés en deux, Nom de dieu!
Fous les églises par terre, Sang-dieu!
Et l'bon dieu dans la merde, Nom de dieu!
Et l'bon dieu dans la merde.

It's heady stuff all right, but it has nothing to do with my grandfather. It all started one day in the car, when, having invoked Eugène to establish control of a couple of bedtime situations, my children asked what he sounded like. Theirs is a world of YouTube and MP3s, in which you can record, save, download or otherwise bank anything, so they expect to be able to hear him at the flick of a switch. What did he sound like? they want to know. 'Sut oedd ei lais, Dad?', what was his voice like? By way of answer I played this CD, and told them that it was their great-grandfather singing. They had no reason to disbelieve me (children don't to begin with), and listened enraptured by the sheer daring of what was being proposed. When I eventually admitted to them that I had made it all up, that the voice was not Eugène Lejeune's, I realised that a part of the original claim remained lodged in their minds like a splinter and would never leave, that the association would always be there.

You can't unsay anything, you realise. In a world where you experience things finishing all the time, irrecoverable – buildings, events, people, happenings – all gone to dust, to the great 'Ubi Sunt' factory of memory, the things you've said seem to stay, long after they were true and even if they weren't. I too have come to make that association, so that Eugène comes back to me whenever that song of anarchy and deicide that has nothing to do with him fills the car.

My grandfather was no anarchist, and really he had no politics because deep down I think he believed in the inevitability of the kind of life he had, in his work and his illness and in his place in the world. Things were there to be assented to and enforced, or rebelled against and changed. My grandfather, even when he was fit and well, wanted as little to do with either side of the coin – assent or revolt – as possible. He refused promotion three times because he didn't want responsibilities, and then retired early for health reasons. Lucie held that against him, that he wanted a quiet life. They had no sort of relationship I can grasp: they rarely spoke to each other, slept apart, flared up into arguments that were always held, like dialogue in Racine, in transitional spaces – hallways and corridors and staircases. The phrase 'stand up row' comes to mind, but only because these two contrived to argue in places with no seating. Lucie was distantly related to the man who had killed Eugène's father (see below: 'Murder in Morocco'), and perhaps that was a source of contention, but most of the time they were cushioned from conflict by indifference.

My favourite story of Eugène's, and I think it may have been his only story, which I asked for over and over whenever we passed Cordemois bridge, was about Pato, whom my mother and Eugène rescued from drowning after he had been put in a sack, ballasted with not enough bricks to sink, and thrown from somewhere near the sewage works upriver.* Pato was a black mongrel who became old and tetchy and died in his late teens, and was fed, in keeping with a family diet which is both a homage and an invocation to diabetes, on cubes of raw sugar. Even Pato, a hairy mongrel so black and messy that his face could not be distinguished from his backside, had a past glory I had missed, and which was always alluded to in order to contextualise the disappointment we felt in him as children. I knew him as old and grouchy, half-blind and panting sourly in his dotage, always seeping from his mouth, his arse or the drooping sheath of his foreskin. We were too late, because by all accounts he had been a riot of young animal, affectionate

---

* Another disappointing thing about Eugène at the time, and which I now admire and wish I had respected, was that he was an anti-raconteur in a world of exaggeration. Many interesting things happened to him, but because he was modest, untalkative, and most of what we'd call his personality took place on the inside (that was his *doublure*, really), he told his stories, when he told them at all, with no fuss and no drama, and always positioned himself on the periphery of anything that happened, even when it happened to him. The story about Pato is a case in point: the first time he told it, he gave a reasonable if slightly Spartan account of the drama of the drowning dog who became a family pet. Other grandparents would have done a better job. When asked to repeat it, he would leave out more and more, betraying the children's need for an inflated Disney-style story, until by the end he would simply jut his chin out towards the water where the dog was saved and say 'Là'. Other old people, compendia of embellished anecdotes, would have been busy adding to the myth; Eugène stripped it down until it became less than it had been, less than it really was.

and vibrant and full of personality. He was replaced by a pure-bred spaniel called Jato, an animal so stupid that even as a puppy we gave him a wide berth, and who died of heatstroke in a car because Johnny, in whose care he was left while my aunt worked, had gone to a café and left him for hours in the sun with the windows closed.

Two memories of Eugène still hurt to call back. The first is that he once took me on the most disappointing fishing expedition I've ever been on, and that I was petulant and angry with him for it as we walked back empty-bucketed from Cordemois bridge. The second, which haunts me, is that he was banned from writing to me when I was at school, because his grammar was poor and he was only borderline literate, even by Lejeune standards. It was thought that this would be a bad example to me in my new situation.

Centenarian

There's an old school photograph that keeps turning up in *Le Cercle d'Histoire de Bouillon*, where the same photographs and reminiscences keep turning up anyway (this is why we keep reading it, for the sameness laid over change), which shows a class of boys with the legendary *maître d'école*, or 'mwéte d'école', as the *patois* goes: the schoolmaster, Lucien Chevy (1872–1951). All the old people remembered him, and he taught many of them, looking thirty years older than them even when he was little more than five years their senior. He is suited-up and stern-looking, with a moustache like the curtain drape in an opera house. At the centre of the front row is my grandfather: moon-faced, with big sad eyes and a beret with a little badge on its front. The photo is undated, but I'd say he was about six, and not yet an orphan, which means the picture is from about 1918. Behind him are his two future brothers-in-law, Emile and Albert Nicolas. I'm not sure where Paul is, the only one I knew well. My guess is that he was truanting, practising the black-marketeering skills that served him so well after the war. Emile died in a fire in 1940 after a bombing raid, while Albert, known as Le Pichalit, a *patois* corruption of Pisse-en-lit, or bed-wetter, moved about fifty kilometres away, and was rarely seen again, perhaps because of his nickname. It's like in Thomas Hardy novels: if you move to the neighbouring county, you may as well have gone to live in Patagonia, so cumbersome to cross and mind-stretching to imagine these tiny distances become.

In the back row, third from the left, is André Millard, one of the hostages the Germans took in reprisal for Edouard Degrelle's assassination. Fourth from the right in the middle row is the already highly slappable face (it would only get more so) of Maurice Pirotte, who has just – 3 January 2013 – turned 100, and is Bouillon's poet.* Too frail to slap nowadays, he is still cheeky and irreverent and even under the tartan blanket that covers his legs and the rims of the tyres of his wheelchair has the manner of a wizened skirt-chaser, from whose lap we might still expect to see a creaking erection stirring gauntly beneath the plaid.

Pirotte is an extraordinary character: a limited poet who perfected his limitations until they became as charming and graceful and hard as enamels. He only ever wrote about women and Bouillon; women as if they were Bouillon and Bouillon as if it was a woman. But it works. In its time and place, it works very well, its mix of sensuousness and abstraction, words like 'soul' and 'void' and 'infinite' sharing line-space with 'breast' and 'lips' and 'thighs', and covering all the bases a normal person would be interested in if they still thought poetry could do the job. 'Je suis un homme pour qui le monde visible existe', said Gautier, in response to accusations of poetic abstraction, 'I am a man for whom the visible world exists'. Pirotte is never far from the flesh, and was also skilled with ink and watercolour, often scripting his poems with a thin brush, accompanied by a quick sketch of the castle or 'Les Ramparts' or a woman with long tresses that segued into the Semois. He knocked off these poems

* Maurice Pirotte died on 18 April 2013, while this book was in production.

in the manner of an absent-minded genius (a pose he rehearsed diligently), was never without pen and paper and ink, and gave them out to people – thousands of them on people's walls and in their drawers or in their scrapbooks. He was the nearest Bouillon had to a bohemian, a dandy of the static community.

My uncle Guy is a believer in Pirotte, and published a handsome 'Selected' of his in 2009, to which I wrote a brief introduction-cum-homage. Pirotte wrote a famous – locally famous I mean – poem about the 'ruelle du passage', the slate-walled alleyway that divides Lucie's house from Guy's, and which continues as a steep cobbled path up to the castle. It's where the Lejeune men used to piss when they were feeling lazy, which was often, and where bats hung all day and darted in and out of at night. Pirotte wrote his poem onto a piece of flowery wallpaper left over from Guy's bathroom makeover in, I think, the early seventies, and Guy framed it and put it up at the entrance to the *ruelle*, where it has stayed all this time. It was probably the first poem I read, and always stumbled at the first word: 'Ici'. Like a character in a Beckett play, I've always found the hardest words of all to be *here* and *now*, and Pirotte has a small but important part to play in my malady of time and place.

The other names on the photograph I also know, because they're all still here in some form or other, even if the people who inhabit the names are long gone: the Serson brothers live on in their grandchildren's 'mazout' firm, which delivers the heating oil to Rue du Brutz three times a year; the Damilots, the Thibaults, the Parentés, the Sinnesaels and Dieudonnés are all still in Bouillon, and their children and grandchildren still carry the nicknames like genes. Only Pirotte

is the last of his line, since he never to his knowledge had children, and he is still here, a hundred years old, surrounded by the long dead who are to him always freshly dead. His business, he says, is more and more with them. In the *ruelle* there is now a sculpture dedicated to him, a hand with a quill writing a line by Pirotte onto a blank page.

MURDER IN MOROCCO

Not Morocco, Africa, but Morocco, Bouillon: 'Le Maroc'.
Parts of Bouillon have names from across the globe. If the
world is a small town, the reverse is also true: hence in
Bouillon we have Le Maroc, La Tunisie, L'Abyssinie, L'Algérie,
Le Congo, and other places associated with French and
Francophone colonialism. The town is parcelled up into the
local exotic, while local differences dictate behaviour and
attitudes. The nearer you live to others, the more different
you have to be from them. In this obsession with being like
nowhere else, Bouillon is like everywhere else. 'Narcissism of
marginal difference', Freud called it, the prizing of small
differences until the differences themselves became the
identity. Three hundred metres outside Bouillon is the hamlet
of Curfoz (227 inhabitants). 'Paysan d'Curfoz' is a Bouillonnais
insult for people who display boorish or crass behaviour. I've
been called it for a variety of uncouthnesses, from going to
the shop dressed only in pants (excusable: I was only eight)
to drinking Coke with frogs' legs (I was forty-two).

The part of town known as 'Le Maroc' is the last suburb
before Curfoz, and housed the lowest-paid workers. It is still
the area where the highest unemployment is concentrated.
Morocco is built on the slope out of town, and the streets are
so steep a tyre could roll itself from one end to the other. The
Lejeunes lived in a small house at the top of the Rue du Lion
d'Or, the first street in Morocco. They were one of three Lejeune
families living nearby, and are not to be confused with Hippolyte

Lejeune, known as 'le Polyte Lolote', and his wife Maria, known as 'Djô-djô', or with Marcel and Joséphine Lejeune, who lived on the same street, and were known as 'les Bë'.

Emile Lejeune had two sobriquets: Emile Picard and Emile la Petite. No one knows why. Father of Olga and Eugène, Emile was my great-grandfather, and he was murdered, stabbed by a neighbour, for letting his pig eat some potatoes the neighbour had put out to dry on a wall. The presence of semi-tame but plate-destined livestock was something I caught the end of in my childhood, so I can faintly recollect what it might have been like to have pigs and chickens and rabbits. Le Maroc, like many of the poorer parts of Bouillon, is still full of rabbit hutches, and if you pass the gardens you can see the hutches and catch their whiff of wet fur, mouldy feed and piss-sodden straw. My grandparents kept pigs until the early sixties, and rabbits until the late seventies. On Mondays, Eugène or Julia would yank a rabbit out of its hutch, kill it with one brisk corkscrew twist of the neck, flay it to its blueish plum-coloured stretch of newborn baby-skin, and hang it next door to a twist of bluebottle-encrusted flypaper until Sunday, when it would be jugged and slowly cooked with prunes, its liver either eaten as a starter or added to the stew to deepen it up.

The murder of Emile la Petite was big news, and is amply covered in the local paper, which can be researched in the town archive. I'm relieved to read that there was a history of bad blood between Emile la Petite and his murderer, and that, however much his murderer may have over-reacted, he didn't over-react so much that he killed a man for the sake of a few *canados*, as they call potatoes around here (see below, recipe for *Canados aux Rousses*).

I imagine a short nasty fight with stubby knives, not the fighting knives you get these days, but the sort everyone carried around back then: to cut your food, peel your potatoes, get the grit out from under your nails, keep in your pocket or in your belt. Push into your neighbour's kidney. Eugène and his sister Olga grew up fatherless. Olga left Bouillon and went to France. She lost touch with Eugène and no one knows what happened to her. Eugène married Lucie Nicolas-Bourland, and moved up to Rue du Brutz, the last street before the castle. They had three children: Monique, Collette and, fifteen years later, Jean-Pol or Johnny.

Emile la Petite's picture is in our living-room, but only because I dug it out from an archive of photos so damp they had stuck together like compacted leaves. He wears a beret, his face is touched up with colour to give his cheeks the blush of marzipan fruit, and his eyes are too close together. He has the air of a small-time trickster, a wheeler-dealer who was always going to come a cropper. The story of Emile la Petite is one I loved as a child, and my children love it now. Why? Because of the disproportion of the offence to the punishment. That's what sets us off dreaming: disproportion, that whole anarchy of cause and effect that reminds us how fast things spin away from us; how much, in the train of sequence and consequence, the instant can open up and swallow the whole life that lay ahead of it.

'AU PREMIER'

In some rooms it is unthinkable to do anything other than whisper. My great-grandmother Julia's room was one such place, and it has taken me the thirty-eight years and the several refurbishings since her death to get used to speaking normally in here. It is still the room where quietness happens: I write here, I'm doing it now, at an old sewing-machine table from Lucie's workroom, and the children repair here when they are overwrought or want to read or doze.

Julia's room had been furnished in the 1890s and last decorated in the thirties, though in a style that deferred to the 1890s. I don't mean *belle époque* 1890s, the kind I study at university and write about: all Mallarmé and Laforgue, absinthe and can-can and Toulouse-Lautrec. No. I mean religious-provincial-industrial 1890s. Crucifixes, brown wallpaper, and furniture so big it had to be built inside the room it dwarfs.

It was wallpapered with a dark, off-burgundy velvet flock, its pattern so dense that the room pulsed. There was a heavy Walloon oak dresser, a Voltaire armchair in which Julia sat reading her *missel*, a brown chaise longue and a round table with two chairs where Julia ate her meals. There was a crucifix on every wall and an elaborate trinketry of religious bibelots on every surface: Lourdes water in plastic Virgin Mary bottles, bone-china saints, antique devotionals jostling with the purest Catholic kitsch: plastic Padre Pio plates and Jesus statues with crowns of fairy lights. Rosaries were everywhere, and even today the things keep turning up, coiled up like millipedes inside matchboxes, on windowsills, behind radiators, in old biscuit tins and bedside tables. Julia went to church three times a day, and when she was too old the priest visited her most afternoons. If I ever imagine my missing Irish childhood, it involves some very similar décor, though less silence.

Julia was utterly devout and seemed to have been planted in the nineteenth century despite having lived through most of the twentieth, not just because of the wooden clogs she wore, one of which is still in the understairs cupboard, but because of the values that flowed up through her. She was illiterate, and had worked as a chambermaid in the Hôtel des Ardennes from her early teens to her late sixties. To think of her, born in the 1880s, living in the house with Johnny and overhearing his Rolling Stones and Beatles records, gives me the same slightly heady feeling of temporal overlap I used to get when, as a child, I watched Westerns which featured both horses and early motor cars, the horses tethered beside parked cars outside a saloon or a bank. Julia had lived through both wars, lost one son to German bombers and waited five years for another to leave Stalag XIII, and spent World War Two in an internment camp working the fields for the Vichy French. On her lap, or kissing her face, it's the mix of chasmic distance of experience and comforting physical closeness I remember. Julia was a warm monument, a statue with flowing blood.

Her body was tall and bony and her face, creased like a pickled walnut, had a wizened serenity that we children found delightful. What I remember most about her was how, when I went into her room, she would get up slowly and smile with a radiant toothlessness, and as she rose keep falling back very slightly before pulling herself up again, as if she was unsticking herself from the shadows. Her room had a special kind of time, and her body obeyed it: slow and curdled, there was a thickness to the minutes. But whenever she went downstairs to make coffee or 'trempinette' (see below), she adapted to the sprightly time of the ground floor, the place of movement and commerce and busy-ness. At these times she was fast, nippy, like a 2CV threading its way through congested streets. The house had its time-zones, different trains of life.

My sister can't remember this, but I can: my mother picking me up after a swimming lesson in Paris, and telling me Julia had died. This is why I associate Julia with the smell of chlorine, the muffled acoustics of swimming pools (voices, splashing, klaxons), and the difficulty of putting on clothes when your body is damp.

RECIPE: *CANADOS AUX ROUSSES*

'Fwére fonre des bouquets d'lârd bin crôs dins ënne cass'role en fonte. Y fwére dorer des échalotes (ne ni les léchi grèyi). Mette les canados pèlés (côrnes de gade, long-plats), les léchi bin dorer; voûdî d'l'éwe d'zous l'couvercle'.

'Sweat a few pieces of fatty bacon rind in a cast-iron pan. Fry some shallots (don't let them burn) until they're soft and translucent. Add your peeled spuds (you can use pink fir apples or any long flat potatoes), and cook them until they're golden; drain them using the lid.'

The recipe calls for a splash of beer and a sprinkle of chicory to give the desired russet colour.

TREMPINETTE

Trempinette is the Bouillon breakfast, eaten by generations and still holding its own against the croissant, considered a new-fangled and effeminate Gallicism, and breakfast cereals, which have yet to reach here. Here is how you make it:

Take yesterday's bread and slice it into strips (the day before yesterday's will do). Place bread into your *trempinette* bowl (a 'djatte'), and add a couple of sugar cubes and a knuckle of butter. Re-heat yesterday's coffee and milk and pour into the djatte. Your *trempinette* is ready when the bread has swollen and floats to the top of the bowl. It is sipped hot from the rim or eaten with a soup spoon.

The key to a good *trempinette* is staleness, the 'yesterday-ness' of the ingredients: the bread must be dry and starting to harden, and the coffee must be on at least its second re-heating, so that its bitterness stands up to the sugar and the melting butter. The true Bouillonnais will not stand for fresh ingredients in their *trempinette*, and I love it for the way it makes use of the unfreshness of things. It is a relic of a period when nothing went to waste. Now, people actually save the fresh bread and the new coffee and put them aside so they become sufficiently stale and old to make *trempinette* from.

We all do this with our food, and with more than just our food: we choose the main attraction less for itself than for the pleasures we know we will get from the leftovers.

Hors sol

The only time I heard my mother talk lyrically about something other than her disappointments was when she described the different ways she liked eating endives, or *chicons* as they are called here. There were many – raw in salad or as a salad to themselves, wrapped in ham and cheese and baked, boiled and then caramelised in butter. Endives are grown 'hors sol', outside the soil, and are intensively cultivated for a Belgian population that *per capita* consumes, so the surveys tell us, more champagne and more endives than anyone else in the world. The Belgian *chicon* is grown in two stages: first the root, which is forced underground and then lifted out, and then the taut bulb of leaves, which is grown indoors in containers once the root has been transplanted into sand and left to sprout and fatten without light. It is the vegetable of displacement, transplantation and – if the word exists – regrounding, which is the same as ungrounding, which may also not exist. And the phrase *hors sol* has always attracted me – when the old people talked about growing things *hors sol*, I was puzzled, asked myself how that could be. The *chicon*'s leaves are heavy and white, tapering to crêpe-thin frills of green that hesitates on yellow, and that damp, shadowy, depressive sourness we like so much is the taste of darkness that has been translated to our plates.

TROIS GANTS

Trois gants was the local *gendarme*. 'Three Gloves' they called him, with that Bouillon gift for the sobriquet. The story I was brought up on was this: to the 50 per cent of Bouillonnais who thought he was omnipresent, and resented or admired him for it, it implied that he had three hands. While to those who believed that he was a lazy and unreliable slacker – in other words the other 50 per cent – it implied rather that he was all glove and no hand. Both of those stories are good, though they are untrue. But I keep them in mind: like my grandfather and 'L'bon dieu dans la merde', they are stories that cannot be untold, unsaid, unremembered, so they linger at the edges of the true. I have since learned, after asking Claude and Guy and a few other old Bouillon hands, that the real reason he got his nickname was that he always clutched a third glove in his gloved hands when he attended ceremonies and functions. It is a beautiful detail of petty functionaridom, an image from Gogol or Flaubert via Monsieur Hulot, and even better than the two stories it displaces.

Though his effectiveness was much debated, nobody disputed *Trois gants*'s ubiquity. The Lejeunes, the Adams, the Fellers, the Bourlands and the Nicolas, inhabitants of 8, 10, 11 and 12 Rue du Brutz, were among the 50 per cent who thought *Trois gants* was useless. Like a character in a Marcel Aymé story, putting his amazing gift to singularly unambitious use, he could be doing nothing in several different places at once: dozing on a bench on the esplanade, queuing for chips on the ramparts, drinking beer Chez Polydanias or pissing it back out at the Estaminet. Modern politicians make big claims for the deterrent effect of a police officer's simple presence, but this would have come as big news to many of us in Bouillon, for whom *Trois gants*'s policing was so 'light touch' that his work could have been carried out by a modest breeze.

I have only one memory of Three Gloves bestirring himself in the direction of law enforcement: during the 1976 heatwave, he once walked down from the Cordemois bridge to the riverbank and ordered my father to cover his shoulders while he was swimming.

DEMOLITION

There's something mellow and almost lackadaisical about the way they demolish things here, as if they were trying to make the pace of destruction match, more or less, the pace of building. It's a kind of symmetry they're after, as if they wanted to right the wrong that it is easier destroy than to build. When I lived in Bucharest in the Ceauşescu era, demolition was frenetic, unpredictable, violent in its execution and intent. It was all about humiliating the past, not just abolishing it.

Here in Bouillon it's more a kind of respectful attrition. The municipal lorries and cranes seem to be chaperoning the old hotel towards its end, drawing its end out of it, naturally, rather than imposing it from outside; the wrecking balls don't so much demolish the buildings as wear them away, and appear to be engaged in euthanasia rather than murder. The diggers stand with their articulated arms hanging, their jaws slack and nosing at the ground like Meccano dinosaurs grazing on the rubble. It took the best part of a year to knock down the Hôtel de la Gare, and even now some of it still stands. It's fascinating: two thirds of the building is a tumbled detritus of bricks and breezeblocks, piled on top of itself so high you can climb it until you're at the first floor of what remains of the hotel, which you can enter either through the balcony, which is intact, and whose French windows are open onto a spectacular view of castle and river, or through a door, which is ajar, which swings in the breeze, and which leads onto a corridor still decorated with paintings and in which you can see, dimly, an old console table with plastic flowers and a decorative Chianti bottle with half a candle in it and a stilled spread of melted red wax. Built in the seventies, the place carries the seventies inside itself, and there's something intimate and nearly sexual about the deep maroon darkness of the corridor: that crowded wallpaper, burgundy flock, with its relentless pattern of tendrils and fist-sized flowers, the mass-produced paintings, in plastic gold frames, of Hawaiian sunsets . . . And above all you notice this: that in all the time the building has been empty and open, parts of it unwalled and ceilingless, no one has bothered to steal anything: the pans and plates and cutlery are all still in the kitchen, the bedding is still on the bed, layered with ten years of dust. Some beds are made, some unmade. The keys still hang from the wooden box behind reception though most of the rooms are air, and the counter still sports its rack of old flyers for tourist attractions. One of them is a fold-out map of the town framed with adverts for long-gone businesses and cafés, titled 'Bouillon, Perle de la Semois'.

If you squinted, you'd think the place was being built, not pulled down.

SOBRIQUETS

For many families, the nicknames are so powerful that their real names wither away from disuse. With some nicknames, person-specific ones such as 'Le Dènn', 'Paprika', 'le Patate', 'Le Pichalit', 'le Zygomar', 'Mataba' etc., the sobriquet shadows the real name for a while, before taking over the job. This is like a handover period, then the real name disappears and returns one last time on the death certificate.

With family nicknames, les Pistache, les Bë, Les Pointës, les Qué-Qués, Les Cassoulet, and scores of others, the children are born into them. My uncle Guy, in reality a cousin of my mother, has always been called Pistache, but so have his two brothers Francis and Jacky, so were his father and grandfather, and so, now, are his children and grandchildren. These nicknames are different. They are part of a numinous inheritance, a link back to the past, and they function as another sort of memory: through wars and across the borders of countries and centuries, up and down the ladder of social mobility, through emigrations and homecomings, through intermarriages and extra-marriages.

Among my favourite of these are a family nicknamed the 'Remplaçants', the Replacements, so-called because generations ago one of their forebears was paid to do military service in place of a wealthy man who bought himself out.

The closest example to me of the generational nickname, or the heritage nickname, the nickname as heirloom, is Guy's aunt and my grandmother's cousin, Nanette (Germaine), sister of the executed Victor, Guy's father. Nanette married an American GI in the liberation of Belgium and went to live with him in Clairton, Pennsylvania (the setting, though not the filming location, for *The Deer Hunter*). Her son and daughter, monoglot Americans – one is a therapist, the other was a Republican Congresswoman and Senate candidate – remain Pistaches, and are always thus called when they visit. It doesn't matter that one sells tantric self-help to business leaders and the other stood for election to the Senate under Reagan and George Bush Senior: when they're here they're as much Pistaches as Guy or Jacky or Francis.

Nanette sits in the courtyard and chats with her school-friends. She visits every couple of years or so, but is too old now – her last visit was in 2009 and she is nearly ninety. She looks and sounds exactly like them, though by some paradox which when you think about isn't a paradox at all, she sounds more Bouillonnais than they do. Her accent is pickled like Degrelle's, preserved. It makes sense: she left, it stopped. She may live in a state-of-the-art condo on the Florida seafront and volunteer for an environmental group that saves rare turtles from the ravages of developers, but Bouillon-wise she's still a Pistache and it's still 1945. Her contemporaries and school friends from the Athénée and the Institut Sainte-Marie wear densely-patterned, stain-friendly housework-proof dresses and black aprons with zipped-up grippy fur-lined shoes. She wears a lime-green tracksuit and trainers white as a film star's teeth. But she speaks in thicker, more *patois*-flecked French than they do.

To imagine what her life must have been like, the bereavements, the geographical changes, the emotional and cultural adjustments, hurts the mind. Realising, as I always quickly do, that more people, on balance, have this than don't, and have it harder than she did, are more lonely, more violently transplanted, and transplanted from violence to violence, are more disorientated and bereaved and alone, hurts even more, and I have to stop. As the man in Proust says about his dead wife, when asked if he still thinks about her a lot: 'Yes, a lot, but only a little at a time.'

Bouillon is what demographers call a static community. Nanette left, but in some ways, for all her travelling and transplantation, she is more static than those who stayed. The exile is always defined by their leaving, but also, for themselves and for others, by the frozenness of the moment of their going. Nanette brings her own stasis to the static community, and for a moment as I watch and listen to her, the roles are inverted – she is rooted in place and time and we are the ones spinning away – and suddenly everything tips over and spills everywhere: here, there, now, then, her, us, spreading uncontrollably along an endlessly smooth floor.

TELEPHONE

Lucie's house was the first on the street to have a phone, and between the early fifties and the mid-seventies it was the only one. Many people on Rue du Brutz didn't have a phone of their own, so used Lucie's to make or receive their calls.

It's a heavy wall-mounted black Bakelite affair in the dark end of the L-shaped corridor, next to where Lucie worked. Before it was disconnected by Belgacom it would make a strange high-pitched gulping sound when you lifted the receiver, which sat on its switchhook like a dumbbell on a squat rack. The phone was inconveniently positioned – you couldn't sit as the lead was too short, so you had to stand throughout. It was mounted with a piece of wood on which there was a hook, so that you could answer the phone, establish who was being called, hang the receiver on the hook and then walk around the house shouting for them to come down and take the call. Wall-mounting was deliberate on Lucie's part, to stop people from lingering in her hallway, and to give that transitory public-phonebox feeling to anyone who might be tempted to settle in. It had a sluggishness and dormancy about it, and everyone I've known who has used it has always spoken a little more loudly and little more slowly than normal.

It stayed connected – same line, same phone – until 2005, and with that disconnection ended all its boxed-up stories. That's what it is: a strongbox for stories. What conversations must have passed through it. Osian and Mari unhook it, and I see their hands sag a little at the surprise

of its weight. 'Plastic?' they ask. Sort of, I reply: Bakelite, Polyoxybenzylmethylenglycolanhydride, the first plastic to hold its shape after being heated, which is just as well, given some of the things I've heard being said into that receiver. Bakelite was invented by a Flemish scientist, Leo Hendrik Baekeland, in New York. Baekeland, the son of a housemaid and cobbler, also invented Velox photographic paper. He sold Velox to Kodak for three quarters of a million dollars, and then made many millions selling his Bakelite company to Union Carbide. He became remote and eccentric and paranoid, ate out of tins and never left his mansion, then died a recluse in 1944. He is buried in Sleepy Hollow cemetery in New York. This phone never received calls from New York, or indeed anywhere in the United States, one of the few places my parents were never sent, but it received them from the Congo (Belgian, as was), Tunisia, Venezuela, Iran, Romania, Turkey, Algeria, France, Spain, Italy, Hungary, Poland, Bulgaria, and of course Britain. It is the best-travelled phone in Bouillon, possibly in the province, and you'd have to go to the Belgian Foreign Ministry in Brussels to find a receiver that has had the static from more countries flowing through it than this one.

This is the phone I called several times from my house in Oxford, where I then lived, as Lucie lay upstairs dead in the bathroom doorway. I had been calling her all the previous day, but there was no answer. She always answered. Her conversation was a catechism of small complaints and expansive endearments, but she always answered. There wasn't much to them, but these conversations are never to do with their propositional content. They're all in the talking, the exchange of voice, the there-ness and the way the there-ness gets channelled down the line and through the narrow aperture of time we have to speak together. There-ness works with silence too.

Why was she not answering? There was only one place she generally was: in the living-room at the back of the house. I called Guy, who said that, yes, she had been down there but had now gone upstairs for a sleep, as she wasn't feeling well. Everything was OK. I was reassured. That evening and all the next morning I called, again and again, many times, and there was no answer. I knew that Johnny and Marie-Paule would be coming to take her on a tour of the 'Home', and thought perhaps she was making herself scarce or pretending not to be in. But no: she was dead. Guy found her. He hadn't seen her making her morning *trempinette* in the kitchen, so he let himself in and went to look. There she was, lying where she fell. She hadn't made it to bed the day before, and still had her clothes on.

That was the phone we used, my mother and sister and I, when we left Iran during the revolution and my father had stayed on, like many staff, an extra few weeks until things became too dangerous. I was in school, watching the Iranian revolution on the news by teachers' special dispensation: the only boy in school who had to watch the nine o'clock news to find out how his parents were. Eventually my mother and sister were evacuated, and I was brought back to join them in Bouillon, where we would all watch the news on RTBF and see the revolution unfold on our screen. Lucie would be at work on a dress, *clientes* would walk up and down the corridor, Eugène would peel his *canados* in the kitchen or pop out to The Arse, Johnny would be listening to the Beatles

('Les Béâtles', Lucie called them) in his room, and Claude and Collette would drift in and out of the house asking for news. Sometimes the phone would ring and it was my father, faintly calling from Tehran, saying things were all right, which was his way of saying they weren't, with us standing in a line in the darkness of the corridor, holding the phone, tangled in its lead, passing it from hand to hand. That phone seemed miraculous then, and it still does, which is why I've left it up on the wall, and despite the fact that I have the latest iPhone and can not only request real-time Twitter updates on any number of revolutions currently unfolding, but I can probably call both the regimes and the regime-changers and ask them how they're doing.

Marie Chenot was an old lady who lived three doors away, up the *ruelle du passage* that began at the back of our house. When we were small, my cousin Patrick and I used to bring her items of shopping and she would give us 'Petit Beurre' biscuits that were always slightly soft, impregnated with the cellarish dampness of her house. Her house was tiny: one up one down, as many of the workers' houses are, with an under-stairs toilet and a cellar for *mazout*, the heating oil many houses converted to after the war. When she became too old and ill, she had the bed brought down to the kitchen, and her life was a tightening circumference of bed, toilet, oven, TV. And then simply bed and TV. I know the people who live there now: they've spruced it up and turned it into a modern *gîte*, but in Marie Chenot's time it was thick with darkness, and she would sit in her armchair and watch television eating cakes and biscuits and *trempinette*.

This was her sorrow: Marie had a child out of wedlock,

and her life as a single mother was difficult until she found a man who, as they say, 'took her and the boy on'. He was a brute who drank, beat her, gave her three other sons, and victimised the boy she had had before she met him. He would chase the child around the street with a knife, threatening to cut off his cock and balls, beat the boy and humiliate him sexually – always sexually – until one day, at the age of eleven, the boy pulled the knife out of his hand and stabbed him in the guts with it. The stepfather survived, but with much-reduced mobility and capacity for evil. The boy was sent to the equivalent of a borstal near Saint-Hubert. His only contact with his mother was through Lucie's phone, because every Sunday for the next seven years, without telling her husband, Marie Chenot came to Lucie's house and phoned him.

PICTURE AND FRAME

This story probably means nothing, but it has the outward neatness of a parable along with the inner messiness that made parables necessary in the first place:

In the early 1990s, I arrived in Brussels with a bag full of Christmas presents. I had forgotten to buy anything for Lucie, so I stopped in an arcade and bought a picture frame. She liked photographs, and the house is full of them, going back more than a hundred years. The earliest frame in the house contains a smudgy photograph of a Bourland in military uniform (he must have moved his head slightly as the shutter came down as one side of his face melts, Francis Bacon-like, into a smear) heading off to the Franco-Prussian war. It is carved with a small huntsman's knife out of dark oak unevenly gouged, though not so unevenly that you can't see a pattern to it. The newest is a shiny red plastic frame with a picture of a recent child.

The frame I gave Lucie was walnut, and had that marbled, rippling wash effect you see on fresh conkers. Inside it, though I didn't notice it then, was a picture of two people, wholesome and bland and with the kind of consensual good looks that seem to have been designed by a focus group. This is how shops sell you frames: there's a standard-issue picture inside – usually sunsets, couples or cats – to show you that the frame works, and also because it would be spooky and unsettling to have a blank space inside it. So here we had a couple, smartly dressed, generically in love and all in all a good advert for people, monogamy and frames. I gave this to Lucie and she admired it and thanked me and said she would keep it in her bedroom.

I never asked what she put into it, and I never set foot inside her bedroom, but I would be lying if I said I didn't assume that it would be a picture of me or my sister, or the two of us together. When Lucie died and I went into her room to clear it, I saw that the frame was there, splendid and polished, but also the picture inside it, which she had never taken out. For the remaining seven or eight years of her life, she had slept with a mass-produced picture of two strangers beside her bed.

I had given her a frame, but she had received a picture.

EVERYTHING AND NOTHING

Where to begin and where to finish? And then, if you've answered that question, you then ask yourself: *whether* to begin, *whether* to finish. The writer who wants to write about nothing (Flaubert's dream of the 'livre sur rien' . . .) and the writer who wants to write about everything are equally doomed, but at least the one who wants to write about everything can make a start.

Watched by Animals

The Ardennais, and the Walloons generally, are fond of animal parts, not just for eating but for home decoration. A great deal of my childhood was spent beneath the quizzical, slightly ironic expressions of wild boar, owls, deer and foxes, whose heads were mounted on the walls of pretty much every house we visited. Of all of these it is the stuffed owl in Mme J—'s house that still haunts me, and is still there, though she died nearly twenty years ago. The owl is in mid-swoop, joining wall to ceiling as it flies out at us from a wallpaper of fat green leaves and flowers. Which of us is more surprised, you or me? it seems to ask.

Animals would be stuffed and put on dining tables or dressers or above televisions, and their skins could be ordered from the butchers' along with the flesh and bones they had once wrapped. Before the abattoir was converted into a sports centre, you could get the skins and heads, hooves, antlers, horns, tusks, legs and tails and have them made into everything from rugs and lampstands to key-rings and bottle openers by a local shop which specialised in hunting and fishing equipment and cheap taxidermy. The animals were there not as hunting trophies – there is nothing boastful or exultant about the way people hunt here – but as guests, albeit dead ones. Their presence, especially against those dense wallpapers with their foliage and tendrils and organic patterns, was like a homage to the forest, an overlap between the woods and the home. In one house I recall there was half a deer that

seemed to spring through the wall, its head, antlers, and a good part of its torso mounted on wood and with its legs in mid-leap. Many of the poses, like this deer and like the owl in Mme J—'s, were thrillingly dynamic, so you got the sense of movement suddenly stilled, and ready to resume, as if the animal was waiting for you to leave the room to complete its action. It was a static safari. Other animals were more dormant. One boar's head just lolled sideways out of the wall, as if the animal had pushed through, taken a look around, and then fallen asleep or died of apathy between worlds. For the hunters, these animals meant something precise: they were, however still and dead, always explosive with the moment of their killing, and therefore with life.

One morning in the woods when I was about eight, I saw some antlers poking through the mist and then disappearing. There was no body, just these ethereal pale branches of bone moving slowly against the mist-muted greens and browns of the forest. The next time I saw a pair of wall-mounted antlers I thought I knew what it was that humans were trying to replicate: that feeling of being watched in return, tracked down in our own habitat, our walls no longer solid but porous and cracked and splitting at every join and angle to let the outside in.

The Golden Boot

There is very little to link my father's family and home, the McGuinnesses of Wallsend on Tyne, to Bouillon, and I often wonder what my father made of the place when he arrived, engaged to my mother, and what my mother made of Wallsend when she visited, engaged to my father. My grandfather on my father's side worked in the shipyards. Like Eugène, he died young, but really very young: soon after my father started at university. My father's mother, Edith, worked in a large department store in Newcastle, and she died when I was about eight. My father was an only child, and it was clear he loved his father and was at best ambivalent about his mother. My mother was not ambivalent about his mother: she disliked her for being a snob (my mother despised the under-resourced snobbery of the self-hating working class), and for thinking that no one, least of all a Belgian, was good enough for her Kevin.

When she died, Edith left me – just me, not my sister – her two-up two-down terrace house in Wallsend. Soon afterwards it was compulsorily purchased and demolished, and my parents spent the money on a small plot of land in 'La Ramonette', the part of Bouillon where the poet Charles Van Lerberghe lived for a few summers writing his long Symbolist poem 'La Chanson d'Ève'. It was the plot next door to my great uncle Paul's house, and it lay vacant until my parents sold it, unchanged but overgrown, twenty-five years later. The only sight I got of my grandmother Edith's house was on some sort of planning document my parents received where the whole street was ringed for bulldozing. I remember being fascinated by the odd way in which houses were represented on architects' drawing or on title deeds: their rooms tightly angled, the diagrams of stairs and roofs, the walls appearing as lines between houses and between house and garden, house and street. It was the way the mess was contained by lines, the way the endless overlappingness of things translated into these fictions of mathematical angularity and unbreachable borders that I liked. But I only liked it because it wasn't true. The different colours too: yellows and blues and pinks, dotted lines like sutures and thick lines like furrows. The houses looked like square amoebas with their see-through membranes.

All of my father's world is lost. He was not especially attached to it, that's for sure, but also it simply couldn't compete with Bouillon; he accepted that and fell in with it. There was an aunt Gladys of his in Cullercoats, someone called Norman in Whitley Bay, an elderly couple called Brenda and Reg who lived in Stafford and then Doncaster, but nothing and no one to draw us back to his world. There was also a family we visited a few times, cousins again, who lived in a large caravan and moved around the north of England. We visited them near a motorway in Bradford, and then again, much later, around Nottingham, before losing touch. They were, I realise now, what are called 'travellers': my sister admired their caravan and I admired their daughter, Peggy or perhaps Pegeen, who was a little older than me and beautiful. My father inherited his mother's snobbery and her clinically nasty tongue, which meant that he despised his own family in ways that corroded him more than he knew. Bouillon was spared that, because, despite the opportunities for snobbery it offered, it always offset them with its eccentricity and exoticism.

So it is always with a sense of a rich but sudden connection, an overlapping, that I see the plaque on the wall on Les Ramparts, the street in Bouillon with all the restaurants and take-aways. It's a plaque with a shiny golden boot, in honour of Philippe Albert (1967–), the great Belgian international footballer and legendary Newcastle defender (1994–99). His face is also carved into the slate and he wears, as he did at the peak of his game, a mullet and a moustache that must have been modelled on the Dalton Brothers in Lucky Luke. Though we knew each other a little as children, I've met Philippe Albert twice as an adult: once in a café in Bouillon, and once in the urinals of the New Inn nightclub in Bertrix, the Manchester of the Ardennes, as no one calls it. We were introduced by my cousin Patrick, who knows everyone, and Philippe bought me a beer. He had just started playing for Anderlecht and I had just started a Master's degree on Ezra Pound and French Symbolist poetry. That was not the only difference between us.

At Newcastle, under Kevin Keegan, he became a cult hero, and Newcastle fans sang a song about him set to the tune of Rupert the Bear: 'Philippe, Philippe Albert, everyone knows his name'. Keegan was himself a cult hero in Bouillon in the seventies and eighties: Kevin Qui Gagne as we thought he was called. In fact we thought 'Qui gagne' was another of those Bouillon nicknames. This cult is linked to a spate of Kevin baby names in the area and, for all I know, across half of Europe. Suddenly there were Kevins everywhere: 'le petit Kevin' you would hear as people stopped their prams and showed off their newborns to their fellow-Bouillonnais. Men with names like Alphonse, Marcel, Léon and Polydore, and women with names like Albertine, Micheline, Germaine and Josette suddenly found themselves with grandchildren called Kevin.

Philippe Albert lived the dream. He signed for Newcastle while Kevin Qui Gagne was manager, which he still remembers as his happiest time, where he played with drive and tenacity, and where, despite being a defender, he was often to be found in the opposing team's penalty area. His goal for Belgium in the 1994 World Cup against the Netherlands triggered street celebrations in Bouillon where his parents were lifted onto people's shoulders and carried around the roundabout on Place Saint-Arnould, where traffic police in white gloves and fluorescent batons serenely misdirect the cars when the crowds descend upon the town. I know Philippe's brothers better, who work in the local supermarket, and I still see his parents in Frank Istace's La Grignotte chip shop (there's a plaque there too: Frank is a member of the guild of artisan-chipmakers). Though there is no plaque to this, Philippe Albert thus represents the link between my father's and my mother's people and places, a small hinge between two panels that meet only in the hinging.

Philippe Albert now works near Bertrix, where he runs a small fruit and vegetable business. He makes his own deliveries early in the morning, and by midday his work is done. He does a spot of commentating, works hard and spends his time with his family and friends in the place where he grew up. Asked why, given the money he must have put aside, he has chosen to drive fruit and veg around Wallonia every morning, he replies that a man who retires at thirty-three needs a bit of routine and that getting up early is one way of staying focused on what's important in life. Sometimes, the secret to a good life is that there is no secret.

EMPTY COURTYARD

Speaking French to my children I think of it now as my
   mother's
tongue if not, any more, my mother-tongue. It's freighted
with a kind of loss; hers, mine, and what she lost as she
   passed
it on to me, continents away from where she started:
shot through with gaps, mothballed and moth-
eaten at once, the smell of preservation neck and neck
with the smell of death.   Lying for years in the cellar,
it fattened up, grew milky, slow, echoed in my mouth
as in a wind-tunnel of its own disuse. Then, like drinking
from the source, came our annual summers in Bouillon,
where our Belgitude rose up in us like the damp
behind the wallpaper in the house that stayed unused
nine months out of twelve: its empty rooms,
lost cupboards, the stored-up junk piled up so long
that each forgotten item now dovetailed into the next,
a perfect carpentry of abandonment; the tongue
and groove of unused words, life in suspension, ready
to rise again like dust in the backdraught from a closing door.

There's something in it when I use it here brings back
those moments when, mid-play, I'd nip indoors for a piss
or for a sandwich and when I came back out the other
children were all gone, the courtyard empty, the toys

back in their boxes and the sky already crossed with
    evening;
brings back the knowledge, always wrong but always
    knowledge,
that there would never be another time than this,
this ending-tainted perpetuity.
                                Now my children taste it,
the empty-courtyard French I used to speak;
they push their tongues along the language
and as I hear their words snag I hear my own again,
and wake from that recurrent dream in which I'm always
waking up, and break off that aborted first line
of my story, that I'm much younger and still Belgian.

My Mother

How I think about her now is how
a thought is said to *cross* the mind:
like a bird's shadow as it flies,
dragging its span in darkness along the ground.

THE BOUILLON HISTORY CIRCLE

The title's well-chosen, because that's how the place comes
    back at us:
in circles, the same tides breaking on the same shores,
    with,
at best, some different waves. It's the places first: boxed up
in photographs, your finger tracks them through the
    decades,

stitches in a tapestry: the football club in 1946,
the primary school in 1917, the Saint Nicolas parade of 1892
   . . .
Here's the horse-drawn carriage for Brussels via Namur
standing in the square – 1908, just as the new station opens

fifty yards away to a crescendo of brass and bunting.
One world segues into the next: it's gone in next year's
    photograph,
as have the mounds of horseshit, which means the
    allotments
by the river (1915)

look underfertilized, the trenches straddled by thin sprouts,
old postbags where the endives sweat, drinking moonlight
through the canvas.
        As for the people, their nicknames chose them
years ago, are more theirs than their own DNA:

Le Dènn, La Bédji, Les Pistache *en famille*, Zizi (*le, la, les*
depending on sex or generation), Maccabi, Le Cassoulet
and his womenfolk Les Cassoulettes. Then a drum roll
of surnames from before the Franco-Prussian war:

Polydanias, Molitor, Sainthuile (always Arsène), Lagalice,
and always (1899, 1920, 1942) a visual sepiatone
refrain, the Pator-Bodard children bent like saplings
under their almost palindromic name.

The *patois* still runs through the Brussels-filtered, Anglo-
    studded
Euro-French: *la mwéjon, le tchinisse, vouille* and *yauk*:
it's the line of dirt that outlasts the soap, the grit
that variegates the marble. Turn the pages and their voices
    rise

from the stapled gulf of photocopied paper: their breath
so close now it's like they're there in front of you,
the smell of beeswax, lathe-oil, overheated radiators,
pot-au-feux and table beer. That's *The Bouillon History
    Circle*,

the quarterly publication of – who else? – the Bouillon History
Circle.

THE OLD STATION

No train has stopped here since the fifties, but it remains
in all the ways that count my stop. It still says *Gare*
above the arch, the *guichet*'s glass has stayed unbroken,

the tracks are gone but there's a kind of stitching
in the ground, parallel scars where grass shrinks
back from growing. Then, kerbside vertigo:

that two-foot drop from platform-edge into
the next arrival, its endlessly suspended service,
and a few (never so aptly named as here, now, though not
   in French)

railway *sleepers*, hold all I've ever known, in miniature,
of the world's speed and its solidity, a delirium of lost
footing followed by the knowledge there was nowhere

further I could fall. This is still the *quartier de la gare*,
where the rain comes down like credits on an old film,
a roll-call of lost professions: slate-cutter, gamekeeper,

sommelier, market-gardener, butcher's boy, seamstress,
blacksmith, breeder of rabbits and dole-queue *flâneur* . . .
the last being my grandfather, tempering each day to a fine
   point

on the soft anvil of his idleness. *Artisan du temps libre*
he called himself, *artisan of the empty hours*:
filling his days of worklessness in the Café de la Gare,

then hollowing out his nights in the Hôtel de la Gare;
he never made his mark on anything
and yet I see him everywhere.

'LA V'LÀ, TA PIÈCE'

The first time I heard – and then listened, really *listened* to – a conversation that was going nowhere and had no intention of ever going anywhere, was when L'Oncle Paul and his wife Marie came for lunch, as they did most Sundays. Paul was Lucie's brother, and a few years older than her. There were three brothers: Albert, or 'Le Pichalit', who now lived in Gaume and was rarely seen in Bouillon; Emile, who died in the Allied bombing of 1940; and Paul. Paul was a wheeler-dealer. He was lucky enough to have been caught early in the war, and spent nearly five years alive in Stalag XIII rather than dead, or worse than dead, in battle. That was where he learned many of the skills that stood him in good stead later, when he became, by Nicolas-Bourland standards, well-off. This isn't saying very much, but by the time he died he owned two houses and a holiday chalet he let to Flemish tourists who went everywhere dressed only in pants,* a small pine wood

---

* I can't remember which of the old Bouillonnais it was – Zizi? Mataba? Paprika? – who once defined the Flemish as 'des allemands en slip', Germans in pants, but I still think of it as I see the tourists descend on Bouillon at weekends in their camper vans and mobile homes, or with their holiday-home DIY stacked in trailers. The invasion jokes have always been there, and Eugène once told some German tourists who stopped him on the Pont de Liège and asked him which way the castle was: 'même qu'en '39', he replied, same as in 1939. I call it an invasion joke, but Eugène wasn't joking.

for Christmas trees, and hundreds of rabbits which he sold, along with his vegetables, at markets in Belgium and France. It was at Stalag XIII that he learned gardening, animal-keeping, and black-marketeering, and when he returned to Bouillon in late 1945 he took a job at the Hôtel de la Poste as an errand-boy cum waiter. Stalag XIII was made famous by the film *Hogan's Heroes*, and though the little checking I've done suggests that there was no resemblance between the real one and the fictitious one, Paul would not have been out of place there. Paul made money during rationing with small-time contraband, and saved up to buy a house in La Ramonette, where he and Marie lived, childless, until his death in 1990. Paul looked like a Walloon Karl Malden from *The Streets of San Francisco*, with a nose that resembled a gnarled potato and eyes that squinted humorously at some far-off comedy – perhaps the role he might have had in *Hogan's Heroes*.

Paul talked a lot, Eugène said very little, and Marie and Lucie had nothing in common because they were such similar people. Watching them talk was like watching two chess players who have arrived at the board with the same game plan. Paul would launch himself into market-gardening and rabbit talk, smoking thick wet roll-ups and drinking white port or whisky. Eugène would talk about football, displaying a knowledge of English league football which my parents' friends found impressive when they visited.* Paul wore either clogs or old boots you now only see on actors playing Vladimir or Estragon: spattered, creased, their tongues lolling and their

---

* Eugène was the last man in the family to be able to talk knowledgeably about sport. Two generations later, his Welsh great-grandson Osian, Osian Lejeune-Prys-McGuinness, has taken up the mantle.

eyes half-laced. His suit consisted of unmatching jacket and trousers, tied together with a red patent-leather belt which he'd bought at some sale from a counter doing clothes for large women. Or borrowed from Marie, who was a large woman, with a wide face and vast thick spectacles that were even wider and belonged more on children's TV than on the bridge of a weathered Walloon nose. Lucie was thin and nervy, and Marie, despite her beaming fleshiness, was canny and sharp. Both women were more literate and more numerate than their husbands, and both understood money and how it worked, though each did something different with that understanding. Lucie was generous with it, Marie was tight as Molière's *L'Avare*, though she was also joyful and good-humoured. It was only money she was tight with: with food and drink, the tarts she baked, the drinks she served, the jams she made, and with her time, she was generous and free. Marie was in charge of Paul's money, and we discovered after he died that she had been siphoning most of it off to her nephew, Thierry, in order – perfectly legally – to dodge the Belgian inheritance laws which mean that a childless person's estate is shared between his wife and his own family. This legal circumvention of the law seems to me to be the very essence of the law. By the time Paul died, there was hardly any money, the pine wood, holiday home and the house in Botassart had been made over to Thierry, and there was only La Ramonette house left, where Marie lived until she went to a 'Home'. Marie was alert and jolly until she suddenly wasn't: dementia didn't *set in*, or any of those gradualist verbs we use to describe incrementalism or encroachment; it Blitzkrieged its way through like the Germans in 1939. Now Thierry lives in La Ramonette with his family, lets out the holiday cottage to the children and grandchildren of the people Paul let it to, and manages the pines and the house in Botassart, near the 'Tombeau du Géant', where Degrelle wanted his ashes scattered.

For me, the climax of these Sunday afternoons would come when Paul winked at me, cleared his throat, and got up stiffly and with fart-stifling care. That was my signal. This may have been the climax for Paul too, because throughout the afternoon he had been winking and gurning at me whenever he caught my eye, pointing at the ceiling, his agitation increasing until he could contain it no more. I would leave the room first and wait for Paul outside the bathroom on the first floor. It was not a pleasant place to meet, though it had the liminality appropriate to conspiratorial encounters: a dark corridor flanked by open doors that opened into rooms even darker, one of which framed a toilet in perpetual flush, and which, by five o'clock on a Sunday, had hosted half a dozen pungent and sulphurous deposits and was still hoarding their aromas.

With great ceremony, and putting his finger to his mouth to conjoin me in secrecy, Paul would delve into his pocket with arthritic hands that looked like flesh-coloured gloves that had been filled with differently sized stones. Slowly, he would pull out a sum of money, so small, so exiguously tiny, that the whole transaction's point seemed not to give me anything as such, but to set me marvelling at the disproportion between the gift and the ceremony of the giving. Now that I am older and have my own money, I realise that gap was a beautiful chasm. Back then I tended to focus, if I'm honest, on the wrong end of the process: the twenty-franc note (that too was disproportionate, but on a national-exchequer scale: why have a note for so little money?). Now I realise that I should have enjoyed the ratcheted expectation, the suspense of Paul's drama, and lived inside them more, let them work on me for their own sakes, and not just sat about, as I did, wondering whether I could even be bothered to wait for twenty francs clammily offered in a fug of clashing shit-smells, given that I could be playing outside, or smoking one of the many ciga-rettes that lay about, or eating sweets, or buying Luxemburgish *eau de vie* from the Epécé like my friends Luc, Dominique and Alain, and that ravenous-looking girl from the butcher's, Murielle.

'La v'la ta pièce – téch-te et dis rîn à la Marie', Paul would say as he handed over the cash, or rather this minimalist symbol of cash, patted my head and headed into the toilet himself to park his lunch. 'Keep it quiet and don't say a word to Marie.'

By the late afternoon, no one would be saying anything. They'd talked and drunk, filled their stomachs and emptied their bowels, and now they sat and listened to the clock. I thought of the pendulum of the wall-mounted wooden clock as a slicer – it reminded me of the meat-slicers in the butchers' shops – and at the start of the day, as people milled and chatted and made food, it seemed to go fast, slicing time salami-thin, tight little rondelles of the minutes. After about four o'clock, the same pendulum would be cutting fat fillets of time, while the Bouillonnais refuelled on silence, listened to each other breathing, dozing. A conversation might start but then fade away, the talk became punctuated with phrases like 'Eh oui . . .' and 'Quant on d'vînt vî . . .' (roughly: 'That's old age for you') and 'Pâç què . . .', the kinds of things you say while exhaling ponderously but without much interest in what either you or the others are saying. They would talk about big things – death, illness, decrepitude – but with such casual fatalism that those big heavy words – *mort, decès, enterrement, maladie* – were like balloons being lightly buffeted from one speaker to another, completely devoid of their darkness and weight.

MAYBE EVEN PARIS . . .

Occasionally, someone or something would add a further stop on our branch-line network of provincial achievement, opening our horizons beyond Arlon, Namur and 'maybe Brussels'. For Lucie, the epitome of 'peut-être même Paris', and I suspect the one for whom the term was coined, was Madeleine Ozeray, who was born in Bouillon in 1908 and became one of the great actresses in French theatre and cinema. She played Helen in Louis Jouvet's production of Giraudoux's *The Trojan War Will Not Take Place* in 1935 where Jouvet himself, who became her lover, played Hector. Maurice Pirotte, the hundred-year-old poet of the Semois, remembers the couple coming to Bouillon. They flaunted themselves like Mazarin, he says, lording it over the locals with their Parisian ways. Jouvet's fabled wit cut little ice with Pirotte, and Pirotte claims to have outsmarted him on more than one occasion. It is true that Pirotte was always a sharp and funny man, and as Bouillon humour is the humour of debunking, it is quite possible that he bested Jouvet. In any case, Pirotte says that the real star who graced Bouillon wasn't Madeleine Ozeray but Simone Signoret, who lived here during the shooting of *Against the Wind*, a film in which she plays a 'plucky' Belgian resistance fighter (see 'Against the Wind').

Sometime in the seventies, Ozeray bought the house next door to my uncle Claude and my aunt Collette, 13 Rue du Brutz, and right opposite Lucie's house and Guy's next door. It was a modest house but with marvellous views overlooking the forest and river. When Ozeray died in 1989, Claude bought it from her estate and intended to knock through and incorporate it into his own house. Knocking through was always a concept I liked, the idea of breaking down partitions, of extending and pushing on, adding room to room, the pleasure of seeing the new space – another room, perhaps just sky or street, outdoors or another indoors – emerging square by square in a smoke of dusty plaster and falling brickwork. But they never knocked through in the end; Claude just used it to store his wine, put in a new freezer, keep his lawnmower, and set up a small studio where, after retiring from the French air force, he learned to paint watercolours.

Ozeray's house was a peculiar place: some rooms were in perfect condition, while others were dilapidated and looked beyond repair. It was open all the time, always unlocked, and since it shared an unfenced boundary with Claude and Collette's house, my sister and cousins and I used to play inside it. Some rooms you could move into there and then, others were derelict. One floor had carpeted stairs and pictures along the stairwell, the other had no stairs at all, or a staircase that just stopped as if it had suddenly changed its mind. It was plumbed in and the electrics worked and we used to mow the lawn on Ozeray's electricity. My memory of moving through the house was of rooms so freshly decorated and so, in spite of it all, *lived-in*, that you thought there was someone there, and of other rooms so wrecked and mouldering that they radiated death and distance. It was there that I first had the thought of the mind as a house, and of memories as rooms: some so fresh you could move into them, others gone and rotten and empty.

There was a large loft where Claude and Collette planned

on making me a *garçonnière*, a bachelor pad, where I could impress Bouillon's young ladies with my cosmopolitanism. I did invest this fantasy with a great deal of thought, not to say detailed aspiration, especially in my early teens, before the darkness came and people started dying, becoming depressed, old, broke or ill, and before I myself started to think, wrongly but for a while strongly – a facet of my schooling, my craving to break away, my Anglification as well as my Anglicisation – that Bouillon was an anchor-drag, a slow, shingly backwater of mind as well as place. In my head I furnished the loft with a black hi-fi, an expensive colour TV, some flashy abstract art, and a drinks cabinet and bar. There was certainly a bed, and there may have been a pool table and jukebox too, because the whole place was straight out of adolescent central casting. The décor was *Miami Vice* by way of Cardinal Mazarin. When I last saw the place, in 2009, just before Claude moved out, the loft was exactly the same as it was when, thirty years before, he and Collette were laughing and joking about turning it into my first home.

Now Claude has left Bouillon, Collette is dead, the house has been split into two lots and sold to two lots of strangers, and for all I know that loft is still as it was. I think of some parallel universe – it's hard not to in Bouillon, some-times I think the whole place is parallel universe – where that adolescent got his *garçonnière* and did it up just so, played his music and shot his pool and brought back the most deli-cate flowers of Bouillon's damselhood, but saved his best form for the rougher ones. He'd be forty-four now.

NATURALISATION

Simenon, a Liégeois (my parents met in Liège: my mother a student of Classics and my father an English language assistant) of prodigious writing speed (seventy words a minute, eight novels a year, two hundred books over a lifetime) and prodigious womanising (four thousand he claimed, though his wife cut him down to size on that boast: 'more like three thousand,' she corrected) was asked why he had not changed his nationality the way successful francophone Belgians often did. 'There was no reason for me to be born Belgian', he replied, 'so there's no reason for me to stop being Belgian.' Nationalism by indifference: it's a refreshing antidote to the usual stridencies of belonging. The Belgian writer William Cliff has a poem about boarding a ship at Antwerp to take him to South America. Asked his nationality, he does not say 'Belgian', but instead 'from Belgium' – a small but important distinction, whereby, even if you can be sure the place exists, something holds you back from saying that you're actually part of it.

My mother, born in Bouillon in 1942, became a naturalised British citizen in the sixties, after a stint in the Belgian Congo where she had seen that, yes, there was one place in the world where being Belgian was not a matter of indifference, and where, on the contrary, it brought with it a whiff of danger. My father had been posted there with the British Council. It was their first tour abroad together, in 1960, and they saw Patrice Lumumba in the flesh, the first legally elected post-independence Prime Minister of the Republic of the Congo, assassinated by the CIA with help from the Belgians in January 1961.* In their three years there, my parents slept with a gun and their passports under their pillows. It gave them an obsession with identity documents, passes and certificates that would only become more consuming as they lived in Venezuela, Iran, Romania and other unrest-blighted or sclerotically corrupt places. Even at the end, in their muffled retirement in Raynes Park, SW20, they carried their passports with them to Tesco and the local Co-op. Their days were spent smoking roll-ups, drinking red wine and watching television with the kind of transfixed inattention you find in hospital wards and old people's homes.

Naturalised . . . What, I have always wondered, was that

---

* 'Mais tout ça ne nous rendra pas the Congo', is a sarcastic phrase that was popular a few years ago: 'That's all very well, but it won't get us back the Congo'. It was used to denote something effortful and well-intended but essentially pointless, and brought the Belgians into comic confrontation with the unparalleled grossness and brutality of their country's colonial exploits. Even here, in Bouillon, the ramifications of Belgian colonialism can be seen in a carved ivory tusk and several ivory figurines brought back over the years by my parents and by other relatives from their travels. They used to stand on the mantelpiece in the dining-room, but some years ago the shame of all that sparkling whiteness made my mother take them away and hide them in the understairs cupboard. I open it sometimes as I forage for forgotten trinkets – for trinkets that I know are not there but which I remember with a vividness that trumps their absence and for a moment obscures it – and the ivory blinds me with the darkness of its light.

'ised' doing tacked onto the word 'natural'? This '-isation', as in 'pasteurisation', is a suffix that denotes process, an interference with nature if not denaturing itself, so that when we say 'naturalised' we actually mean 'denaturalised'. But only if we assume that it was natural to have any sort of nationality in the first place. Perhaps Belgians are more attuned to the artifice of naturalisation than anyone else, though I know that the only times my mother ever insisted on being taken for Belgian were when she was mistaken for being French. As Beckett said, when asked if he was English: 'Au contraire.'

THE FACTORY FOR SAD THOUGHTS

Some days I become a factory for sad thoughts: the night shift starts not when I go to bed, but when I decide to go to bed. As I turn the lights out, the factory lights come on. I used to make them by hand, the sad thoughts, but lately it's become more of an assembly line, the machines doing all the work: I sleep, and in the morning I have another consignment ready for distribution; for export, for import.

The last time my mother died, the final time – as she would have said, 'une fois pour toute', once and for all – I was in Tenerife. She didn't speak much even when she was alive, so was certainly not going to waste the little she had to say on last words. So I had to make them up, not the words so much as the movement of the lips. Because even alive she was hard to read, as abrupt and closed as her father, but more tortured. She was an ocean's worth of storm clamped inside an oyster.

One of the sad thoughts I manufacture is that I am trying to hear her speak but, like in a bad film, the words and the movements of the mouth are out of synch. In the scenario I've constructed – her trying to say her last things to me – it causes me terrible anxiety, and I try to align her lips with the words she's speaking. It takes so much effort that I forget to hear the words themselves, and I'm not even sure they are words and in what language. I've had this often with dreams of dead people: they are saying something and I can't make it out, and so I get closer and closer, only to find it's a dark and ashy language, all muffled, and so low it's almost a growl. If those are the last words, I think to myself (my dream self thinks to itself), I'm not sure I want to hear them.

I could perhaps trace this dream to the fact that she spoke French and was always ill at ease with English. But even that doesn't explain it, because we spoke to each other in French always. Really the dream is about distance. In my dream she speaks, and the words overlap with the lips and then the lips outpace the words. There's the feeling of something lost in the crevasse, and it's all to do with time, with aligning two sets of moments, and I know that if I don't align them I will never hear, let alone understand. But maybe that is all she has to say anyway, all she wants me to understand: the crevasse. What she has to say she will show, not tell.

That anxiety, a tiny trace of it, remains whenever I watch dubbed programmes. Bathos, I know, but today I saw an episode of *Columbo* in Flemish, and had that same feeling of a narrow but deep chasm between the mouth and the words, the after-twitch of lips which have outstayed the words they spoke.

My mother needed subtitles more than she needed dubbing.

Of all the poems I've ever written, this is the one I didn't.

AGAINST THE WIND

One Sunday afternoon at school, when I was about thirteen, we were in the TV room watching, or half-watching, since someone had a bottle of vodka and we were drinking it with the lights out and the curtains drawn, a black-and-white war film whose title I didn't pay attention to. I paid some attention to Simone Signoret, and noticed that one of the British actors in the film looked like that old bloke from *The Professionals*, the granite-faced Scottish one with ginger hair. (I know it's Gordon Jackson, but I'm retelling this as it was felt, in that hybrid long-finished but real-time-unfolding present tense that reflects the inside of our lives far better than those three stooges, the past, present and future.) Something in the film's background caught my eye first, and made me look again, the way your finger along a smooth surface feels a snag and returns to circle it. The setting looked a bit like Bouillon. There were people milling around a square that resembled Place Saint-Arnould, though many of the buildings were destroyed and the bridge was built out of wood. There was a classy-looking façade with one of those slate-clad domes you see a lot of in the Ardennes that looked like the Hôtel de la Poste, and a small quayside with terrace houses overlooking a thick-flowing river.

I stopped what I was doing and started watching. A car crossed the bridge, and then another, into the camera rather than away from it. It was a car chase, and once they crossed the wooden bridge I knew as the stone Pont de Liège, they turned left and headed along the Ramparts. It's Bouillon; I can recognise it, it makes me weak and shaky; I'm choking with a kind of anguish and I try to tell someone but no one is interested. 'That's Bouillon!' I say, 'where I live'; then, realising it isn't really true that I live there, I add lamely 'where I was a child' (I don't say *when* I was a child, which would be more normal, because right now place matters more than time), and besides it's only partly true, since I was a child in plenty of other places too, and really I'm still a child, and I'm here in a Bristol basement watching a war film on a dark autumn Sunday with the taste of dead leaves filling my mouth. The cars speed past the buildings I know, though they aren't what I know them as, then swerve up past the back of our house and Guy's, past the Ruelle du Passage and the Hôtel Du Château Fort, which is still the Hôtel Du Château Fort. From here they can go in three directions: down towards the war memorial which isn't yet there, up to the esplanade and the castle, or down the Poulie and past the bosses' houses. This is what they do: swoop down that steep and narrow little street, and it's my stomach I feel thrown up into my throat as they hurtle down towards the river and Cordemois bridge (also now made of wood) where I swim and smoke *Belga* and loiter, and where I've fished wordlessly with Eugène.

Why do I feel this way at seeing Bouillon on film? It's one of the strongest feelings in my archive of disorientation. But why? For one thing, I want them to stop so I can look around, it's the shock of the speed. For another, I don't want them there, on this screen, here in Bristol now; it mixes places in ways that disturb me, throw me off balance. Why do I feel so desolate and sick? It's the familiarity first: Bouillon looks exactly the same, the town and streets and buildings, the cars sweeping metres away from my mother and aunt, my grandparents, Lucie possibly even then at her window sewing as they filmed, and the whole of Bouillon flaunting its pre-existence, its endless and ongoing pre-existence. It was familiarity of the worst kind, emotional matter out of place. After Cordemois bridge, Gordon Jackson, Signoret and the prisoner they've sprung hurtle down the road to the Epine, and down what I knew to be an eventual dead-end marked with a water-mill but which the film presented as the open road to freedom. I used to swim there with my father and Eugène, and after my grandmother's funeral I went there to skim stones with Yann, my cousin, Johnny and Marie-Paule's adopted Vietnamese son. As this chase unfolds, the Germans are caught up in Bouillon, first by a herd of cows strategically led across the bridge to block them, and then by the film's set-piece: the carnival parade, which takes place on our street, outside our house. The Germans drive up the Rue du Brutz, past the Café Polydanias which back then is still the Polydanias (how can something in the past 'still' be something it is today?), past the church where Degrelle was refused communion by his own parish priest, and by the time it passes 8 Rue du Brutz I feel nauseous and weak, my heart pounds and I think I'm going to faint as they pass my door, then Guy's door, then Georges Dasnoy's front steps at number 12 (it was Luc, his son, who ended up going out with Murielle). In the corner of the picture I can see 11 Rue du Brutz too, Claude and Collette's. There's a mêlée of Bouillonnais faces, child extras carrying candles and an effigy of the Virgin Mary, indignant crones and folklorically faced old men gesticulating angrily at the occupying troops in ways they probably didn't in real life, not if they knew what was good for them. After that sequence the film switched elsewhere, and there was nothing more. A few minutes later, the film finishes and the credits roll.

My first act when the film ended was to ransack my stash of coins so I could phone home and tell them I'd seen Bouillon on TV. I rang Lucie as the phonebox wolfed down my two 50ps, then my tens, and lastly my 2ps. Yes, Lucie said, of course, everyone in Bouillon remembered, it had been filmed in 1946, when Bouillon was still half-wrecked from land and air battles. There was still rationing, the bridges were still destroyed and temporary ones had been cobbled together out of wood, many of the houses were still in ruins. The cast and crew lodged in the Hôtel de la Poste and the Panorama and a few other places around town, and the cafés were full of movie stars. Eugène would be playing *couyon* in the Estaminet or the Polydanias and in would walk Simone Signoret – there's a meeting, well, a non-meeting, that sets me dreaming. Other actors in the film were Jack Warner (of *Dixon of Dock Green*) and James Robertson Justice, the go-to man of the period for gravitas and girth. Lucie had seen Simone Signoret, here playing in her first English-language role, many times, though hadn't made a dress for her, more was the pity, and had even been in one of the shots herself, of the carnival parade, as had Collette (then aged four), and my mother (six).

When I watched the film right through, impatiently, fast-forwarding in my head and with the video remote control, to the bits I wanted to see, I discovered that Simone Signoret's cover was as a dressmaker, and that her transmitter was underneath the same sewing machine that Lucie had in her workroom. Simone the secret agent would sit at her table with her tailor's dummies, lift the sewing machine off its base and send her clandestine messages. Lucie's Singer sewing machines could flip under the table to make space for other kinds of work, so she could write bills or pencil her designs onto tracing paper, and that too was part of the secret lining effect of Lucie's workroom, of that life, of that childhood. The idea that you could be a dressmaker and secret agent too . . . well, that was too good. All those linings, those *doublures*.

'We'll be all right once we've passed Bouillon', says one of the resistance fighters. Bouillon stars as itself, I suppose, as does the SNCB, another of my childhood's reference-points, the Belgian rail system, which comes in for a good thanking in the film's closing credits.

Against the Wind was directed by Charles Crichton and released by Ealing Studios in 1948. They didn't need a set – they had Bouillon, which for years after the war looked like it did during the war. It's not a great film, it has to be said, but the plot is like a crude parody of the reality of Bouillon in wartime, which was I suspect far less glamorous but far subtler. Here it is, the plot I mean: a group of special agents, including a Scottish explosives expert and a Belgian resistance fighter (Signoret) have a dual mission to destroy Nazi files in Brussels and then spring an allied agent from German custody. There is however a double agent among them, a lining inside the lining. There's a standard fare of romance (the deep lack of chemistry between Gordon Jackson and Simone Signoret is worth seeing in itself), betrayal, suspicion and fast-moving armoured-car chases. There are also some fine scenes of Brussels as well as Bouillon. What strikes me is how soon after the war the people of Bouillon would have had to watch the fictionalisation of their own reality. How did they feel, so soon after being invaded, shot at, hostaged, imprisoned, deported or killed, about having their experience turned into fantasy?

The answer is, so far as I can tell from talking to people over the years who remembered it, and from the accounts in the twice-yearly publication *Le Cercle d'Histoire de Bouillon*, that they loved it: the filming, the reminiscences of the filming, and the special free showing which all of Bouillon was invited to when the film was released. The film itself they aren't that bothered about, and it is only of interest to them as a repository of people and places they know, or know are gone. It's a bit like the *trempinette* principle: the leftovers – in this case memory, anecdote, orientation in time and community – are superior to what they are left over from, namely a factitious rush of celluloid. No one seems to remember the story or any of the actors apart from Signoret, and occasionally someone unearths an old photograph of her smoking on the Pont de Liège being ogled by locals or sitting at the Estaminet, found among their parents' or grandparents' things, and sends it in to *Le Cercle d'Histoire de Bouillon* to publish in their letters pages.

Watching the film with my children, who know the places too – they shout them out like bingo-callers, but don't have the fractured internal recognitions I used to have: they are better adjusted, the places of their lives and the lives of their places are in better balance – the film still disturbs me, but not because of itself, or even the flashes of recognition I get as this or that building or street corner or windowsill, lintel, kerb or stretch of knotted water comes into view, but because it pulls me back to that day in school when the real place with its smells and tastes and sights became a celluloid ghost of itself. The next time I phoned Lucie I was told Eugène had died, and that my parents were on their way to Bouillon for the funeral. I was sitting at the payphone wearing brown flared cords I'd found in Johnny's room and wore at weekends, running my finger along the ridges as she talked and as other boys impatiently jangled their change to hurry me up. My eyes were quite full, and I remember the corduroy lines getting larger as she spoke, magnified by tears that refused to fall. *Against the Wind* comes to stand for all films, but only because it is a film of Bouillon; a liquid plaque that stops time only by being made of the same stuff as time, like a statue made of flesh, that preserves things forever at the cost of reminding you that they're gone.

CHASING YOUR TAIL WITH NIETZSCHE

'That which doesn't kill us makes us stronger, said Nietzsche', someone told me after my mother died. Typical that Nietzsche doesn't entertain the third option, of being neither strong nor dead, but numb. But perhaps he means that being numb comes under the rubric of being strong. But then he'd have to admit it also came under the rubric of being dead. In which case he was right: that which doesn't kill us makes us stronger. No third option.

STOLEN SAINT

This recess or alcove (I know the word in *patois*: 'potelle') used to contain a small painted statuette of Saint Nicolas, the patron saint of *miquelets*. It had been there through the twentieth century and some of the nineteenth. The house into which the space is carved, 37, Rue du Brutz, belonged to an old friend, now dead, of my grandmother, and has been derelict for about ten years. It is being 'done up' as a holiday home in a piecemeal and erratic way by someone from Namur who is either too lazy or too irregularly solvent to do more than half-paint a room, half-install some double glazing or half-re-tile the kitchen before disappearing for another six months. 'DIY Wallonia-style', quips the Flemish artist in Guy's 'Les Miquelets' *gîte*, who thinks of himself as one of life's quippers. Like many such houses in Bouillon, it is a ruin in progress, but progress in which direction?

One day I returned for a holiday to Bouillon and found the saint had gone, leaving only this small, sacred vacancy that no one – not the church, not the council, not even the ruling Catholic party and its perpetually-in-power *bourgmestre* – has had the idea of filling. It is coming into its fifth year of emptiness, and sometimes I wonder if I'm the only person who has noticed this.

Mini-Europe

When I was thirteen I was taken to a place called Mini-Europe, on the outskirts of Brussels. Mini-Europe is pretty much what it says it is, an outdoor theme park in its strictest sense: a park with one theme. It is full of small and intricately detailed scale models of European landmarks, each of which comes with copious statistics about its country's population, GDP, industrial output, linguistic, ethnic and religious balance (where there is one) and (again: where it exists or can be explained) electoral system, all presented on laminated roadsign-sized notice boards. Mini-Europe is at the foot of the Atomium, the vast model of an atom which was to be to Brussels what the Eiffel tower is to Paris, but isn't. Both the Atomium and Mini-Europe have educational missions, which is why they're so boring, but together they constitute an interesting pairing, each in its different way symbolising how not to explain things to anyone, let alone children: Mini-Europe makes Europe small, the Atomium makes the atom vast. It's as if in order to understand things all you needed to do was shrink them or enlarge them. Going to the two 'attractions' together makes you feel like Gulliver: first you are a giant scanning a portable continent; next you are a nano-midget in an elevator between the spheres of an atom that has been magnified 165 billion times. In the end both things expose you to the fallacies of inner and outer, that tag-team of fake opposites.

Thinking about Bouillon and my life there, I realise that

Mini-Europe does have its explanatory uses after all: my early childhood there gave me exact and detailed small-scale replicas – technically they were proto-replicas, since the replica tends to come *after* the original and not, as in this case, before – of every major feeling and emotion I'd ever have. With Mini-Europe, you stood outside and looked in at, or over and across, buildings that, when you saw them or felt them in real life, engulfed you and couldn't be taken in whole; buildings that offered you no place or perspective from which to see them clearly. So it was, dramatically, with feelings: feelings and emotions that swallowed me up when I was older and have yet to spit me out, I knew in a kind of emotional pocket-size when I was a child. So that when the real things happened, the deaths and illnesses and losses, the bereavements, divorces and disappearances – in other words when the Atomium paradigm of being crushingly outscaled took over – I was able to recognise feelings that might otherwise have been too big to withstand.

STATIONS

I have written a lot about stations, and about trains, and spent a lot of time in and around them. They are where I do some of my best mourning, and rail travel generally is conducive to all varieties of introspection, from the kind where you feel you're descending a mineshaft to the kind where you feel you're being scattered thinly and lightly, like the ash you will become, over the world around you.

I like station buffets and I like station hotels and cafés, places which seem to have absorbed something of the essence of departure and arrival but not to have caved in to them: the sticky, reluctant going, the fresh confusions of arrival, the empowerments of disorientation, and all that lies between them. The solidity of these places in the face of all that going and coming seems a comfort. There's a muted romance to it all that you don't get in garages or airports or bus depots, but also an ordinariness too, as if all our departures and arrivals were part of a single movement, and we simply have our own piece, hewn off, to work on like a sculptor with a slab of marble.

I like those station cafés that stay open all night, playing to those goods and post trains that go on through, dragging the curves of their sirens across the night, long after the country's passengers have gone to bed. In my mind I transfer those haunted diner scenes from Edward Hopper onto the dark interiors of Walloon cafés. They are reminders that there's no such thing as complete silence, complete stillness, complete emptiness, but it's precisely because they aren't silence, stillness, or emptiness, that they help us to evoke those absolutes. Less is not always more; sometimes it's everything.

These cafés and hotels are also places of intersection: day shift meets night shift; commercial traveller, timetable-squeezed and destination-harried, meets backpacker with no sense yet of where he wants to go. Last night's drinkers overlap with this morning's espresso-randy executives; it's someone's thousandth visit to the town and someone else's first and only one. These cafés and hotels wear neon advertisements for old drinks long since abandoned by the market or still occasionally ordered by grandparents when they remember to. They have their seasonal specialities, limited but usually decent food such as all-night spaghetti or a ham hanging in a backroom that smells of dog food and the damp cardboard of cash-and-carry boxes. In the Arlon area they serve their own Maitrank, the Luxemburgish Mosel wine that has been macerated with asperule flowers, sweet woodruff, which according to the Maitrank website, 'broadcasts its aroma in early May' – hence the name: May Drink. These places keep watch over the stations and are so still you'd think them closed, though they're always open. My favourite old station, aside from Bouillon, was Quartier Léopold in Brussels, which was clean and colonial on the outside, but derelict on the inside; where the trains didn't stop but slowed down glutinously, long enough for you to feel you were inside a dead tooth: a pristine white shell mushy with caries. It is now an information centre for the European Parliament, and the old Quartier Léopold has been mostly knocked down to make room for the glass and steel buildings of Euroland. There are no Bruxellois left in the area, and when I was last there I felt like the only Belgian, perhaps even the last Belgian.

Being only half-Belgian does not disqualify me from that slightly adrift sense of belonging that constitutes Belgitude, because all Belgians are only half-Belgian.

I spent a lot of time in the part of Bouillon called the *quartier de la gare*, where the old station created around it a small eco-system of shops and cafés and hotels. They've long since closed and some are now being demolished. The station was part of the Paliseul-Bouillon *vicinal*, and as it came into town it gave you spectacular views of Bouillon, ridging the hill so you saw the castle, the Ducal palace, the Ramparts and the river. It then wound downhill and across the Pont de France and headed out to the villages and eventually across the border to Sedan. There is still a pair of parallel scars where the old track used to be, and if you compare today with old postcards and photographs of the *vicinal* at its height, you see that the old track and the new lines of blank, grout-coloured gravel correspond exactly. Rail-shaped barren lines are etched into the grass, and the ghost of the old track is still there, faithfully following it, rail-shaped aftermaths of rails in the fat undergrowth.

The *vicinal* shut to passenger traffic in 1957, and then in 1960 to freight trains. When I knew the station it was the bus depot, where the yellow local buses to Libramont and Paliseul grazed on a concrete forecourt. It had lost most if not of all of its stationhood by then, 'essence of station' you could call it, and the businesses that had grown up around it were gone or going in a last-gasping, lingering way. In the peak years of the *quartier* as a place of bustle there were a couple of hotels and a few good cafés, a bookshop, two newsagents and a record and musical instrument shop. The Post Office was also placed there, and today is the only one of those businesses to survive. The station hotel is in the process of being demolished, but it used to be swanky and expensive, the first hotel in Bouillon to have a sauna. The station is owned by the council, and they keep it spruced up in cream paint, though the old bell is still there and looks splendid robed in rust and ready to ring, if there was anything to ring for. From the dark, syrupy carillon of the church announcing a juicy Walloon funeral to the hollow, mothballed jingle of bare coathangers in an empty wardrobe, Bouillon was a town of bells. These days it's mostly the tourist train that you'll hear.

You can go up the steps through the arch where the platforms used to be and instead of steaming trains and travellers and cases there's a flat empty wasteland with waist-high weeds. Nearby, the only café that still works is Le Vauban, run by Willy the landlord who was a mercenary in the Congo, who made good money doing bad things, and is now a slow, shaky drunk who runs a tobacconist's from inside his café and cooks meals for his customers on a camping stove on the bar.

Trains tell you about time, though what they say is never conclusive. At least Belgian timetables do what they say they do: they tabulate time. Here in Britain you get given the destinations alphabetically arranged, and then the time of departure and arrival. Belgian ones give you the time, hour by hour, minute by minute, so you look at the departure time first, and then follow the stops until you find yours. If it isn't there, you look to the next departure. You look through each departure time until you find your stop, and doing so you see all the stops you won't stop at, and many you won't even pass through. Belgian stations are full of people running their fingers along the timetables, often with their lips moving as they speak out the station names, like worshippers at a prayer wall. The train connections are called 'Correspondances', and you see the words emblazoned across the timetables and departure boards.

ANGELRY

I've been attracted to the poetry of train travel, and I enjoy the species of sub-attentive attentiveness it brings out. European train poems are usually about speed and movement, about transport in the sense of 'transport of the soul' or 'transport of the senses'. Even the lulls are enriching, allowing you to look and see and drink in the stops. British train poems are about stalling, or breaking down (Donald Davie's 'In the Stopping Train' is perhaps the greatest analogy between a broken self and broken rail network: 'Time and again, oh time and/that stopping train!/ Who knows when it comes to a stand, /and will not start again?').* It isn't surprising – not since Auden has a British poet really got into the spirit of train travel, and this is partly because our trains are so bad that only nostalgia can give us back the idea of freedom on the rails. Compare that with the exultant optimism of Cendrars's Trans-Siberian Prose (Cendrars was the Kerouac of rail), his idea that you can start anywhere, finish anywhere, but that a certain directedness beyond your ken would always enfold you; or the mysterious, luminous everydayness of modern

---

* I wrote this before I discovered that Davie's 'In the Stopping Train' was written about a train journey from Tours to Paris, and hence only qualifies as a 'British' train poem because of its author, and not its location, train or rail network. This doesn't negate my theory about comparative rail poems, but it does undercut the breezy certainty with which I offered it up.

French train poets like Gilles Ortlieb. Ortlieb has written about the economically depressed French Lorraine, and his position of perpetual unmooring as a translator in the European Commission in Luxemburg gives him unique access to the dignity of this area's desolation. He too is an *hors sol*. He writes about the ex-industrial towns that end in *ange*, that remaindered German suffix (it's tempting to call it, loadedly, German *annexe*) that was the butt of so many wars and is now the butt-end of so much history. His book, *Tombeau des anges*, which won Luxemburg's Prix Servais in 2012, charts his visits through towns that are in reality epitaphs of towns, town-shaped vacuums; that are to towns what a high-water-mark is to water, what the scar is to the wound.

Here in Belgium, in the Ardennes, in the Province de Luxemburg and our own Belgian Lorraine, we have our fallen angels too: Martelange (where my uncle Johnny now lives), Pussemange, Dodelange, Radelange . . . the question is how many angels you can get to dance on the head of a pun. Like Bouillon, these towns are still vibrating from the shock that made them stop. They have stopped; they aren't going anywhere, but they vibrate in their own outlines like tuning forks. Vibrating is not quite the same as moving, and for me, these ongoing vibrations are as meaningful and mysterious and heroic as anything I've felt in the great 'dead' cities of literature: Bruges, Venice, Ravenna, Saint-Malo, all of which have spawned a breed of necro-tourism which, ironically enough, keeps them alive. Not here: these places, my places, are kept authentic by never being looked at, and even now, immersed in them, I have to keep turning away from them in order to recapture the desuetude that made me want to look at them in the first place. How can you convey the unlooked-at-ness of places and things?

In one of his poems Cendrars puns – I am sure he does – on that word 'Correspondance', the idea of an integrated rail and transport system being, as in Baudelaire's poem 'Correspondances', a transcendent harmony of routes, each one different from, but also somehow equivalent to, the others; it's a great holistic dream, something symphonic, great ramifying synaesthesias of steel and glass and iron and wood. As Baudelaire wrote of his 'correspondances', they 'chantent les transports de l'esprit et des sens': they sing out the transports of the soul and the senses. Baudelaire may well also have been punning on rail transport and rail timetables, since we know he was an avid train traveller, and that he used that line from Brussels to Luxemburg when he went to visit his friend Rops in Namur. We know too that after his visit he boarded the train in the wrong direction and finished up in Luxemburg.

The point is, it doesn't matter whether you start in Bouillon or Paris: you can be in Kiev or Moscow or London or Cardiff, and all those places are already there at the end of a rail. Stations start from somewhere so you don't have to. Here in Wallonia the trains always work, and they're always on time. It's the destinations that are late.

TOURIST TRAIN

Napoleon III, who stayed at the Hôtel de la Poste in Bouillon for one night, has little to recommend him, beyond provoking Hugo's *Les Châtiments* and the great line from Marx, which was a refinement of Hegel, about how history repeats itself first as tragedy and then as farce. In Bouillon this is true of the train, which now survives in the form of a clownish repetition: a tourist train that isn't a train but a train-shaped lorry, painted garish red and black and yellow, which emits a camp high-pitched whistle as it drives along the streets and alleys where the rails once were. But the *Petit Train* is no new-fangled *attrape-nigaud* – it's been going nearly fifty years. My uncle Johnny used to drive it when he was back from college, and I once met some motorcyclists in Wales who had visited Bouillon in the seventies and remembered a wild long-haired youth driving the *Petit Train* and jumping drunkenly off the bridges into the river whenever it stopped to pick up passengers. That was Jean-Pol becoming Johnny, down from university in Brussels and earning drinking and smoking money in his home town.

The original *vicinal* began in 1888 and worked for just under seventy years, and by my reckoning the tourist train is well on the way to outlasting it. Père Doffagne passed it on to fils Doffagne as a going concern, and it is a hugely successful enterprise in the brothel of packaged sightseeing that Bouillon's tourist industry has become.

Marx's exact words are 'Hegel remarks somewhere that

all great world-historic facts and personages appear, so to speak, twice. He forgot to add: the first time as tragedy, the second time as farce.' I would add that Marx forgot to add that Hegel forgot to add that the farce would last longer than the tragedy, and that the parody would outlive the original. But that sometimes you have to settle for the farce and the parody because they're the only kinds of memory you're likely to get, the only evidence that there was an original in the first place.

National Day

I'm thinking of those Belgitudinous sallies of self-mockery by which the country makes you patriotic despite itself, despite your distance, your irony towards the country and, most of all, the country's own irony towards you. There are forms of ironic belonging we adhere to in Belgium at a national level, because they are alternatives to the abrasive separatism with which we've been threatened for the last several decades. Patriotism here is definitely a spectator sport, in the sense that there are more spectators than players. It is certainly true that the place was made both by accident and design, and that the two communities – three if you count the German community – have nothing in common and little reason to be together.

The *fête nationale* in Bouillon is unusual for the fact that it also plays the French national anthem, 'La Marseillaise', alongside the Belgian one, 'La Brabançonne'. But already we have a problem, because the 'Brabançonne' is repudiated by many Flemish because it was written in French (the lyrics are in fact by a Frenchman). The last few years I've been the *fête nationale* in Bouillon has been dismally attended. It is held at the war memorial by the river, where the dead of two world wars and one UN soldier from Bouillon killed in Somalia, along with the executed hostages from World War Two, are commemorated on a stele with an iron statue of the Walloon cockerel, a cockerel 'rampant' as they would say in heraldry, on the top. Usually the only people who attend are, aside from me and my Welsh-speaking children, a few tourists, some local politicians who want to be seen by other local politicians, and a handful of old people of my grandmother's generation.

There is a brass band that starts at the Hôtel de Ville and parades through the town picking up followers the way an old clapped-out vacuum cleaner picks up dust: no longer by suction, but by dragging its nozzle along the floor and hoping to engage a few tufts. The fire brigade and police are supposed to attend but last year the fire brigade forgot. National day doesn't count for much when your real sense of belonging comes from the parish, the few square miles you'll cover with your feet in a lifetime where stasis becomes indistinguishable from change.

The most poignant sight at my last *fête nationale* was an old lady, a contemporary of my grandmother's, attending the ceremony while simultaneously pushing and being held up by a tartan shopping trolley on wheels. From it there hung a lucky rabbit's foot dyed in the national tricolour of red, yellow and black, clipped to the rim of her trolley with a clothes peg. I couldn't have put it better myself.

THE BELGIAD

Caesarean state:
every roadsign a mirror
every town a suburb

*

Magritte's Saturn: all rings and no planet

the ever-provisional
coastline dreaming of sea

*

Maigret's Liège stands in for itself
its anonymous crimes
sweepings from the poorhouse floor

Charleroi's slow factories turn like the Ferris
wheel in *The Third Man*

*

Louvain, Gand, Anvers
river-cities face to face with themselves
Leuven, Gent, Antwerpen

*

Bruges one long aftermath, held breath

*

Bouillon to Blankenberg,
Martelange to Knokke
300 kilometres of frontier
united and untied

*

From the citadel of Namur, Baudelaire's Paris
appears in a cityscape by Rops: France doubled,

*

doubly not. The Meuse rolls through
as many names as it has valleys to run dry in.

*

All has that faint emphasis, as if the place were in italics,
could look like elsewhere yet be nowhere else.

DÉJÀ-VU

Two tenses grappling with one instant, one perception:
forgotten as it happens, recalled before it has begun.

AFTERWORD

With this sort of writing it seems important to distrust the material, maybe even to make distrust itself the material.

I once read an article about a tribe of Arabs who had, sometime in the late nineteenth century, invented a set of picturesque traditions for the benefit of explorers and Orientalists who came to photograph them, measure their heads, barter for goods and generally anthropologise them for newspapers and academic articles. A group of elders had been in charge of developing these traditions for the anthropo-tourist market, and when the anthropology season was over, the craniometers packed and the tripods folded, this tribe of inscrutable and exotic 'Others' went back to living a life which, give or take a few differences of climate and diet, looked pretty much like everyone else's. A century later, the tribe still practised the same traditions, but by now they had become real traditions: divorced from their initial cause, they had taken on the authentic mystique of genuine identity-markers. They had become what they had pretended to be.

But it's not just them, it's all of us. Here in Bouillon I have watched small traditions or tribal habits and beliefs – a street festival here, a *patois* phrase there, a local legend or a piece of manufactured family history – change from things you tell or perform or invoke for others to things you tell yourself, that you invoke and perform for yourself in order to be and to remain yourself.

*

In my mind, Bouillon was never changing but never static either, like endlessly falling never-settling snow. Just the idea that Bouillon might go on while we weren't there, that it might have a normality we were not part of, was troubling and melancholy. 'What do pets do when humans aren't looking at them?' my niece once asked me. It seemed as if she'd been saving up the question for me, since I clearly had the air of someone who had been troubled by similar problems.

I remember wondering why things changed all the time, why they seemed to have to change, but never changed in Bouillon. Sameness has its wonders – you just have to eye its static mysteries from the proper angle and with the right apparatus. You have to understand that duration is not measured only by events – though it's by events that we are taught to understand time – any more than life can be understood solely by movement. But how else could it be done? Our attention to events prevents us from comprehending processes, beside which events are just the spume that rides the wave. Then I read Lévi-Strauss: continuity needs as much explanation as change, he wrote. He was right. We were asking the wrong question. Instead of wondering why things changed, we should really have been asking why they didn't.

My mother left Bouillon, then Belgium; my aunt Collette, married to Claude, died childless and my uncle Jean-Pol moved to Martelange on the Luxemburgish border, where he and his wife adopted Yann, a boy from a Vietnamese orphanage who is now grown up, gay, and lives in Brussels; my sister lives in Edinburgh and I live in Caernarfon and Oxford. Our parents are dead. This house, in which scores of people lived and died, ate and cooked and worked and slept, fucked and gave birth and argued and laughed, is empty for all but a few weeks in the summer and Easter. There are no more Lejeunes in Bouillon, and all it took was one generation – one early death, one infertility, and one emigration – to put an end to hundreds of years of our branchline of people and place. Is that continuity or is that change? And does it even need explaining? Compared with the millions of brutal, extreme, violent and tragic stories thrown up by the twentieth century about places and people, this one barely counts.

What I want to say is: I misremember all this so vividly it's as if it only happened yesterday.

Acknowledgements

I'd like to thank various people who helped me with this book, and who, in different ways, enabled me to capture things I thought I had lost, or who helped me find the angles of vision and the ways of thinking and feeling that gave the material its interest: John Redmond, Charles Mundye, Gilles Ortlieb and Sarah Cochran. My children and their mother have always appreciated Bouillon and understood what it meant to me: the fact that I still have it at all is down to their willingness to return with me several times a year and let me marinade, like my ancestors, in the place's Wallonitude. Then there is my family, for whom I have yet to write a book in a language they can read; Claude Feller, Guy, Agnès, Patrick and David Adam, and Johnny, Marie-Paule and Yann Lejeune. No one could wish for better people to have grown up with.

A large part of this book was written in Brussels, during residency in Passaporta, to whom I owe grateful thanks for a reflective stay in the post-national city-state that our capital has become. I am especially grateful to Sigrid Bousset and Anne Janssen: *hartelijk dank*.

I am grateful for permission to reprint 'The Belgiad' from *The Canals of Mars* (2004) and 'Empty Courtyard', 'The Old Station', 'Déjà vu' and 'My Mother' from *Jilted City* (2010), both published by Carcanet Press.

'Doors and Windows of Wallonia' first appeared in the *Literary Review* and 'The Bouillon History Circle' in *PN Review*.

All the photographs were taken by the author.